HAMMER AND BLAZE

Hammer and

Blaze

A GATHERING OF CONTEMPORARY AMERICAN POETS

EDITED BY ELLEN BRYANT VOIGT & HEATHER MCHUGH

The University of Georgia Press | Athens & London

Acknowledgements for previously published works appear
on pages 329–36, which constitute an extension of the
copyright page.

© 2002 by the University of Georgia Press
Athens, Georgia 30602
All rights reserved
Designed by April Leidig-Higgins
Set in 10/14 Minion by BookComp, Inc.
Printed and bound by Maple-Vail

The paper in this book meets the guidelines for
permanence and durability of the Committee on
Production Guidelines for Book Longevity of the
Council on Library Resources.

Printed in the United States of America
06 05 04 03 02 C 5 4 3 2 1
06 05 04 03 02 P 5 4 3 2 1

Library of Congress Cataloging-in-Publication Data

Hammer and blaze : a gathering of contemporary American
poets / edited by Ellen Bryant Voigt and Heather McHugh.
    p. cm.
ISBN 0-8203-2406-x (hardcover : alk. paper)
— ISBN 0-8203-2416-7 (pbk. : alk. paper)
1. American poetry—20th century. I. Voigt, Ellen Bryant,
1943– II. McHugh, Heather, 1948–
PS615 .H33 2002
811'.508—dc21   2002000860

British Library Cataloging-in-Publication Data available

Refining these impatient Ores
With Hammer, and with Blaze
Until the Designated Light
Repudiate the Forge —

Emily Dickinson

CONTENTS

Go back twenty-five years, to Goddard College in Plainfield, Vermont, where a new paradigm in higher education had just appeared, adapting closely supervised independent study to graduate work in creative writing. There you will find the source of this unusual anthology. The program founded in Plainfield continues to thrive at its subsequent home, and from the work of several decades of that program's faculty the present anthology makes its offering.

Our MFA is designed specifically for individually tailored apprenticeships — and unlike the earlier "workshop" model does not require students and mentors to occupy the same residential location. When the community of writers does gather, for two weeks on campus every six months, faculty members have an unusual opportunity for cross-fertilization of our own work: we team-teach workshops, visit each other's classes, respond to colleagues' lectures.* Because the program's range of aesthetics is as wide as its commitment to craft is rigorous, it attracts a group of faculty writers unlike one another in aesthetic style and signature although likeminded in pedagogical purpose. That design, those ideals, and this energizing colloquium still flourish, since July 1981 at Warren Wilson College in Swannanoa, North Carolina, just down the road from Black Mountain, where another educational experiment once established the single aesthetic that bears its name. Our charge, however, continues distinct and undiminished: not to impress on poetry a characteristically collective voice, but to make room for a variety of voices.

Every poet who has taught with the program at Warren Wilson was asked to select for this volume a sample of his or her work; all but four responded and are represented here. The editors, Heather McHugh and Ellen Bryant Voigt, were part of those early days at Goddard, along with Stephen Dobyns, Louise Glück, Thomas Lux, Steve Orlen, Michael Ryan, and others who were writing poems that anticipated, and influenced, the innovations in narrative, lyric sequence, accessible wit, dazzling linguistic surface, and adapted forms that invigorated American poetry in the 1980s. Some joined us more recently, Agha Shahid Ali bringing to the house of poetry delicate ghazals and canzones, Anne Carson her genre redefinitions, Linda Gregerson a precise metaphysics,

Tony Hoagland his wry meditations, Campbell McGrath his inclusive unlineated pieces, Carl Phillips an array of arresting syntactical structures, and Dean Young an inexhaustible gift for invention. For the present volume, most have provided very recent work; others have offered a brief retrospective.

The excellence of this poetry is no secret: contributors have garnered Pulitzer, Ruth Lilly, National Poetry Series, and Yale Younger Poet Prizes; Bollingen, Kingsley Tufts, and National Book Critics Circle Awards; MacArthur, Whiting, Guggenheim, Lila Wallace, and NEA Fellowships. *Hammer and Blaze*, like the program in which these poets have taught and continue to teach, represents a truly broad geography of aesthetics, with ranges as vast as America's own. It also provides an exemplum of enduring commitment to, belief in, and exercise of poetry's exacting craft.

This collection was compiled as part of the program's Twenty-fifth Anniversary Celebration. All royalties from it are assigned to program scholarships, and we thank the participating poets, their publishers, and the estates of Larry Levis, Roland Flint, and Tom Andrews for these contributions. We also gratefully acknowledge the important efforts of Emily Wheeler, Barbara Ras, Elizabeth Tucker, and especially Peter Turchi and Amy Grimm, whose consistent and generous attentions to every detail have made this anthology a reality.

Heather McHugh and Ellen Bryant Voigt
October 2001

NOTE

* Selected program lectures have been collected in *Poets Teaching Poets: Self and the World* and *Bringing the Devil to His Knees: The Craft of Fiction and the Writing Life*.

HAMMER AND BLAZE

In a Trunk Not Looked into for Twenty Years

Snapshots curled in rigor mortis,
cuff links with the emblems of a lodge,
braided hair rings, a whistle, marbles,
hodgepodge of pocket knives, tin tops . . .
and here, Father, is that ringbox
I'd forgotten — in your faded
handwriting three words: *Redbud. Dark red.*

The box holds two small seeds
shining like brown taffeta.

Here in my hand is your shy love for color.
The painter you might have been spoke once
when you told us all the story of a doll
you saw as a boy at a carnival —
how you loved her dress of scarlet silk,
how it shone still on barbs of memory.
You were thirteen, a crack shot.
And you won. No one laughed
at the uneasy prize you chose:
to hold that bright material awhile
before your delighted sisters got the doll.

Flowers you'd bring from hunting trips
would be as dead before you got them home
as any meat you'd shot —
wild orchids we didn't know were rare,
carnivorous sundew, bluebonnets
too blue, bogflowers nameless and scarce.
Sometimes you'd have a branch of redbud

wilting beside you in the truck.
You said it kept the winter back.

Dark red. You'd found a strange one,
deeper colored, extraordinary. You marked the place
and you came back in autumn for the seeds.
You thought I'd want to raise
in my suburban backyard a thing uncanny
as your wilderness kept turning out to be,
where creek banks sown with the teeth of ancient seas
bloomed with furred and pliant shadows,
where the green air turned and turned
its whirligig of birds.

When I was a child, you sketched them all for me,
each creature in its chosen place,
even the serpent curled on a branch, asleep.
I have the pencil drawings still,
bleached but full of detail, primitive
and skilled and wary as the animals themselves
printing their tracks on that preyed-over ground.

Now I've just returned from another country —
the whole Peloponnese was snared in bloom.
At Olympia, the broken columns lay
in a shoal of Judas trees,
the hold of Zeus ashimmer in pink fire.
Redbud. Judas tree. The same
branches of such ill luck they had to bear
the awful dead weight of remorse.
Greek blossoms surged like fountains
among the shattered temples, betrayal everywhere.

I've heard of seeds taken from a tomb
in Egypt, planted in sterile soil, and brought to bloom.
Not here, Father. Nothing's here
but this inheritance: my imagining eye
sketching on a windowpane the strange

vision of a tree like a scarlet skirt
afire among ghosts of the shrinking forest,
suddenly bright
as the spreading blossom of blood you lost,
and desperate with spring.

South Woods in October, with the Spiders of Memory

There's no touch like this one
except (if you remember it) your baptism,
that silent passage through breaking
unbreathable circles of light
where you were caught quaking and brief
in the fingers of clarity.

The world's strung with embraces.

And this air is pearled with a music
far from us but earth-struck
and deep as that water
from which you could wake and wake.

You can never quite see what makes it
to echo and thrum with the taken.

There's just this touch that is not
like a lover's, is more
barely moth-dust and sun-slant,
your eyes new-lashed with it.
You go forward by shudder and wreckage,
bearer of imperceptible message,
brushing the dead from your face.

Cycladic Figure

Better than Brancusi. Nobody has ever made
an object stripped that bare. — Picasso

After the Fall,
after the plummet from pliable green
and lambent shadow, all impression
of the garden vanished. Imprints
of blossom and fruit, entangling vine,
leaf and animal and bird
in their once and perfect forms —
these have been excised.
Exile has pared this image;
implement and need have come.

And the mild, vaporous dawn
that could not die is lost.
Lost, the life on which wild world
engraved itself, blunt kinship
with beasts and stars in that *before*
where bloodshed daily was
unconscious and undone.

Not yet begun: the known,
our waking dream, labor of time
and the mistaking mind.
Soft Minoan frescoes are not quite
imagined. Inconceivable the Attic
art that will be born in grace
and die diffused in ornament.
Languages, philosophies to be caught
in the nets of possibility, faiths
and wars and kingdoms — none is yet.

Luminous, seeming to be made purely
of tenuous light, this figure clasping its own
form is born altogether of earth

that has given such reflection
again into our hands,
a charm, a grave conjecture
thin as the new moon.

This candle we may bear
as we have done before
into the sepulcher.

Renovated Zoo, Now Called *Habitat*

This is their better life, each kind in place
where low walls and cunning moats address
an almost beautiful, almost spacious,
almost accurate wilderness.

Now the lion's breath can feather
great clouds on a larger winter;
the wolf trots longer as he burns
his pattern on this lengthened run;
and we see more of the lustrous otter's
turning into underwater's
sudden turning into glass.

Here's envisioned jungle and savanna,
mirages verging on suburban
where the aging leopard lunges,
and elephants, our lapsing emblems
of the Pleistocene's parade,
in thunder-colored skins go under
imported trees, allotted shade.

On the tiger passant, light and dark engage
to adumbrate an antique cage.
Forward and back, and back, and back,

his roiling stride of silk and rage
mocks the old constricting track.

What comes here after dark? Not ease.
Perhaps the city's nightmare comes
to each of these, and shaped as they are shaped:
clawed fierce-footed if that is right,
beaked and flying if it flies,
or coiled and striking, saffron eyed —
our fantasy assailing as our manufacture takes
them into art and absence and desire.

To Charlotte Brontë

Your teacher's letter, when it comes
at last, seems like another lesson
in conversational French: "It is necessary
that you not write so often. I have not
the time to answer more than two times
a year." You run your fingers over
the fine script, over the raised seal,
as if the touch of ink, of wax, could
bring him closer than words placed clearly,
evenly: pointed and impenetrable as a fence.

In the bare sitting room, watching your sisters
bend their smooth heads over their work —
flies caught in webs of their own invention —
you wonder if you imagined afternoons
in a Belgian schoolroom, speaking a French
you've almost forgotten, delighting
your teacher, whose eyes became pools
that invited you to swim.

You begin a reply: "I am well aware
it is not my turn to write. I will try
to restrain myself." Over a hundred years
later, writing a man, I use almost
your words, my usual speech formal
with shyness. I think of you searching
for the French "restraindre," staring,
as if you'd find it in the moors — gray
and undulating as the waves that keep
England from Belgium, bare as the years

you must fill alone. "Me restraindre,"
you write at last, gripping the pen
as other words — unruly, unkempt,
so like my own — shoulder their way
between the lines: "My life is nothing without you."

Slipping

Age comes to my father as a slow
slipping: the leg that weakens, will
barely support him, the curtain of mist
that falls over one eye. Years, like
pickpockets, lift his concentration,
memory, fine sense of direction. The car,
as he drives, drifts from lane to lane
like a raft on a river, speeds and slows
for no reason, keeps missing turns.

As my mother says, "He's never liked
to talk about feelings," but tonight
out walking, as I slow to match his pace —
his left leg trailing a little like
a child who pulls on your hand — he says,
"I love you so much." Darkness, and the sense
that each visit may be the last
have pushed away years of restraint.

A photograph taken of him teaching —
white coat, stethoscope like a pet snake
around his neck, chair tipped back
against the lecture-room wall — shows
a man talking, love of his work lighting
his face in a way we seldom saw at home.
I answer that I love him too, but
hardly knowing him, what I love
is the way reserve has slipped from his

feeling, like a screen suddenly falling,
exposing someone dressing or washing:
how wrinkles ring a bent neck; how soft,
how mutable is the usually covered flesh.

Persephone

Close to solstice, the sun barely rises,
skims the heads of skeletal trees, and drops —
so early I'm every day amazed. The sun seems drawn
to oblivion, as I, leaving a party, forgot
the friends who waited, and followed you
into the dark. You never asked would I; I
never said I would, walking heedless
into a night of no stars or reason.

Persephone, I think, was drawn like this,
and Hades no more familiar with the dark.
He sensed how she longed to drink of it,
offered the pomegranate, its flesh so like
living tissue stripped of skin, it quivered
on the tongue. She tasted, swallowed —
how could she not? They say clouds wept
stones; Demeter's fury froze even the seas.

Winter's coming seems tragic. But who can say
this night sky — stars' silver apples
filling bare trees — isn't beautiful? Who
can say Persephone didn't love the dark lord,
hadn't grown tired of living with her mother,
safety, endless mildness, all that perfect light?

Full Flower Moon

The moon develops the earth, and prints it
platinum, the sky's grey a bit bluer,
barely distinct against the stars.
Full Flower they called this moon
when people noticed degrees
of bloom, when there was little but blooming
to notice, and all the blossoms
opened in their proper time.
High over the fields, the radio signal
winks its red eye, competing, knowing
where the Northway stretches its coils.

The valley stretches out from here
as if it would never close, the land
still breathing through mouths of clover
and vetch. Beauty is this openness:
your hand that won't turn against me,
the width of your untroubled cheek,
the pollen of lashes fanning across.

We drive out the old hay-track, buoyed
by alfalfa and light, the scent of thyme
released by crushing, the lollop of hills
running parallel, each moving by eons
into its own shape. So surrounded,
we try to say what beauty is, or makes —
our standing awed together here, inundated
by space and shadowless light. And how
when something stretches so open and limitless,
someone who feels himself made small
in comparison will itch to enter,
place his mark on a body so trusting, so
unsuspecting he thinks it will be easy
to make it his own size, as the red eye
gives him its blessing, more constant
than the moon, but bringing nothing to flower.

Up To

And what have YOU been up to?
Someone who's been talking all dinner
about herself guiltily and indifferently
turned to me: *Up to,* as if I'd been
in mischief, or able to undertake more
than the simplest routine, patterns
I could make for myself and be proud
to fulfill. I mumbled the usual mumble
about much work, and so betrayed you,
as surely as Simon Peter denied Jesus —
though I, as usual, wanted to relieve everyone
of feeling uncomfortable, as they might
at any sign of incompetence from me —
mishandling a knife, dropping a glass.
Cool, smooth, civil is how I want
all interchange with strangers, unless
I sense some gap in poise or rougher
invitation. Your death seemed too unseemly
a presence to bring to that polite meal,
and so I ignored you, who would have
pulled up a chair in a torn and oil-stained shirt,
grime in the creases of your broad hands
and in the lifelines, recalling old farmers
unembarrassed by their looks. You'd have
straddled the chair and asked the polite guests
some impolite question — not to challenge,
your curiosity shockingly pure — "Does it bother you
that I'm dead?" you wouldn't hesitate to ask.
Your listeners would shock themselves as their own
truest, least formed questions escape: "What is it
like? What are you up to, where you are?"

Wide-Eyed Look

As fog lowered and lowered the navigable ceiling,
fear made you silent, more competent,
not allowing it to hold you,
flying along rivers and roads through valleys,
around mountains, and I trusted you
in those 50-year-old contraptions
of balsawood and cloth, rocking
as they puttered like child's play
across the sky, trusted you
not just with my life, but my death,
happy to die with you, doing this.

Only once — so steady and sure
were you in a plane — the unexpected
shocked you: the commuter bound for Albany
from Boston crossing our bow at such
scant distance the passengers' faces loomed
at the glass, and you turned to me
with eyes so wide and blue
they seemed overtaken by sky
and all the unforeseen it contained.

We laughed at our luck, but never
tested it again, on the invisible road
of our flight plan. When, on unfamiliar ground,
that Jeep came skidding and leaping
at you, whirling on ice you couldn't
stop on, I wondered how much you knew
in those seconds when no maneuvering
could save you, and whether the wide-eyed look
you'd turned towards me was on your face then:
the look that would have been your last,
amazed that this blacktop with its negligible
coat of black ice — bare fields and silos
the only witnesses — would be where skill
and calm competence, strength and appetite
for life counted as nothing to the unforeseen.

"Some Vision of the World Cashmere"

If I could bribe them by a Rose
I'd bring them every flower that grows
From Amherst to Cashmere!
— Emily Dickinson

I

But the phone rings, here in Amherst: "Your grandmother is dying. Our village is across the bridge over the flood channel, the bridge named for Mahjoor."

"There's no such village!"

"She had a terrible fall. There is curfew everywhere. We have no way to bring her back. There is panic on the roads. Our neighbors have died."

There never was such a village . . .

"We are your relatives from her mother's mother's side. You've heard of us! We once were traders and sold silk carpets to princes in Calcutta, but now we are poor and you have no reason to know us."

II

I put the phone down in Srinagar and run into the sunlight toward her cottage in our garden. Except for her dressing table mirror which Sikander, so long dead, is polishing, the army has occupied her house, made it their dingy office, dust everywhere, on old phones, on damp files, on broken desks. In her drawing room a clerk types. The colonel, dictating, turns around. My lost friend Vir! Srinagar is his city, too, he wouldn't have ordered its burning. It's not him. Someone else with a smile just as kind, the face of a man who in dreams saves nations. Or razes cities.

"My grandmother is ill. Please send someone with me. Please, someone with me in one of your jeeps to the village."

III

In her room the sun shines on her father — a painting from which he stares, unblinded, at even today's sunlight.

Just then through the back gate some villagers and her dead brother are bringing her slowly through the poplars, by the roses. I run out: *Thank God you're alive!* She is telling her brother, *Be grateful you died before these atrocities. My small home a dark office! How will I welcome you?*

IV

The mirrors have grieved in her absence. They run to greet her at the door. It is her home again! Sikander has turned on the radio: a song of Mahjoor's, in Raj Begum's voice: "The whole universe is worth nothing more than your shadow." And I'm holding her hand in that sun which is shining on all the summers of my childhood, shining on a teardrop in which windows are opening, amplifying her voice, and she is telling me, *God is merciful, God is compassionate.*

The Last Saffron

Next to saffron cultivation in interest come the floating gardens
of the Dal Lake that can be towed from place to place.

1
I will die, in autumn, in Kashmir,
and the shadowed routine of each vein
will almost be news, the blood censored,
for the *Saffron Sun* and the *Times of Rain*

will be sold in black, then destroyed,
invisibly at Zero Taxi Stand.
There will be men nailing tabloids
to the fence of Grindlay's Bank,

. . .

I will look for any sign of blood
in captions under the photos of boys,
those who by inches — after the April flood —
were killed in fluted waters, each voice

torn from its throat as the Jhelum
receded to their accounts and found cash
sealed in the bank's reflection.
I will open the waves, draw each hushed

balance, ready to pay, by any means,
whatever the drivers ask. The one
called *Eyes of Maple Green*
will promise, "I'll take you anywhere, even

in curfew hours," and give me a bouquet —
"There's a ban on wreaths!"

2

    I will die that day in late October, it will be long ago:

    He will take me to Pampore where I'll gather flowers and run back to the taxi, stamens — How many thousands? — crushed to red varnish in my hands: I'll shout: "Saffron, my payment!" And he'll break the limits, chase each rumor of me. "No one's seen Shahid," we'll hear again and again, in every tea house from Nishat to Naseem. He will stop by the Shalimar *ghats*, and we'll descend the steps to the water. He'll sever some land — two yards — from the shore, I, his last passenger. Suddenly he'll age, his voice will break, his gaze green water, washing me: "It won't grow again, this gold from the burned fields of Pampore." And he will row the freed earth past the Security zones, so my blood is news in the *Saffron Sun* setting on the waves.

3

        Yes, I remember it,
the day I'll die, I broadcast the crimson,

• • •

so long ago of that sky, its spread air,
its rushing dyes, and a piece of earth

bleeding, apart from the shore, as we went
on the day I'll die, past the guards, and he,

keeper of the world's last saffron, rowed me
on an island the size of a grave. On

two yards he rowed me into the sunset,
past all pain. On everyone's lips was news

of my death but only that beloved couplet,
broken, on his:

"If there is a paradise on earth,
It is this, it is this, it is this."

(for Vidur Wazir)

Ghazal

Pale hands I loved beside the Shalimar — Laurence Hope

Where are you now? Who lies beneath your spell tonight
before you agonize him in farewell tonight?

Pale hands that once loved me beside the Shalimar:
Whom else from rapture's road will you expel tonight?

Those "Fabrics of Cashmere — " "to make Me beautiful — "
"Trinket" — to gem — "Me to adorn — How — tell" — tonight?

•   •   •

I beg for haven: Prisons, let open your gates —
A refugee from Belief seeks a cell tonight.

Executioners near the woman at the window.
Damn you, Elijah, I'll bless Jezebel tonight.

Lord, cried out the idols. *Don't let us be broken;*
Only we can convert the infidel tonight.

Has God's vintage loneliness turned to vinegar?
He's poured rust into the Sacred Well tonight.

In the heart's veined temple all statues have been smashed.
No priest in saffron's left to toll its knell tonight.

He's freed some fire from ice, in pity for Heaven;
he's left open — for God — the doors of Hell tonight.

And I, Shahid, only am escaped to tell thee —
God sobs in my arms. Call me Ishmael tonight.

After the Auction of My Grandmother's Farm

My father has secretly taken up whittling.
He's hollowed a piece of pine into a box
and inside I find tiny, unfinished toys —
lopsided tops, and snowflakes, small as jacks,
with missing points. The wood is so soft
I could press my thumbprint into it.

A long winter is coming. You can tell
by the way the hogs huddle silent in their pen.
I stand on a bowed gray slat of their fence
and they don't even look, their curved white backs
lined up like dim eggs in the failing light.

In my grandmother's house an artist
is at his easel. His canvases are everywhere —
all larger than himself, and all the same:
paintings of a doorframe open to darkness.
The room is only doors. I walk out

pass the swaybacked barn, past the mailbox.
A moonlit dog trots toward me — silvered dust,
his eyes the color of water. And then a man appears,
my grandfather. I know him from dreams —
his smile, his slouch hat. He opens the pasture gate.
The dog bounds ahead of us, into the posted woods.

Chequamegon

I know how not
to tell this. A dented can
held freezing water from the lake.
It was like washing our hands and faces with fire.
Think of sterno scent, of
coffee grounds. In the van,
upholstery peeling off the seats.

We stopped somewhere
for tools and groceries.
Walked into a reservation bar
to ask directions. The darkling rusted
swivel of that place.
Its heavy door.

It was April, ice
still edging everything.
Each breath a drink
of well water laced with tin.

We climbed a fire tower,
wind splintering through its metal grids.
Later we stood on a pier
as narrow as a gangplank,
the blueblack wince of the lake
glinting all around us.

In the woods I let him say
his words. They sounded
like leaves, years and years
of leaves.

But this is where
I get lost every time.
The bare trees. What I didn't do.
His ghost laugh loose above me,
red strip of cellophane snagged

in the grass. When we walked back
half of the trees we passed
were marked for cutting — yellow bull's-eyes,
a slapped splash of suns. I followed him,
you understand. I disappeared.

Chronic Town

If I listen to that year now,
it's a traffic song in winter, the gray hum
of the skyway arched over eight broad lanes,
the metal rattle of the freight lift in my building.
I lived in a converted nurses' dormitory —
pocked cinderblocks, mattress on the floor.
Green floors and walls, the air itself washed through
with the faint sweet green of convalescence.
Whole families lived in some of the rooms —
taut pierces of Chinese or Korean through the walls.

I'd found work in scholarly texts and reference
in the basement of a college bookstore.
We had a dying customer, George,
who always asked for me. His mother
would wheel him behind the counter,
and I'd bend down close to take his order —
mathematics, linguistics, Russian novels.
Two or three words could ride out on each breath,
but barely formed, almost inaudible.
It took all my concentration to hear him.
When he'd leave, my throat would be tense from trying
to grasp and shape each phantom word.
From trying to speak for him.
The shallow wind of his voice would tremble
through me all day, medicinal, floral.

• • •

Nothing to go home to,
I'd walk that icebound city into dark,
the threadbare shadows of my small griefs
wrapped tight around me.
And would lose myself in the ghosted streets
until the cold pressed through and drove me inside.
In the library the homeless slept upright
at long tables, gripping their open books.
I'd sit there listening to the slow scuff
of my own heart, the useless letter
it kept rewriting. In my pocket a scrap
of paper, pressed into my palm weeks before
by a deaf customer whose fierce signs I couldn't read.
An intricate glyph, a treble clef in barbed wire —
the buried title of every book he needed.

Imaginary

Kalispell last night, a highway payphone, he dialed her number.
Recognition slanting her voice like the trace of an accent
she had tried to lose. *Who is this?* she had repeated into the static,
then colder, quieter, *Who is this.* And him not answering,

just trying her name, the small shape of it, saying Would you please
talk to me, ice-rough rain slicing through, until, after a few long minutes,
she hung up. He's sure she'll think but never believe it was him,
not after all these years, and the black cloth of distance, the weather's erasures.

Carpathian Frontier

. . . like something thoughtlessly,
Mistakenly erased, the road simply ended.
— Larry Levis, "The Widening Spell of the Leaves"

A foreign street, a crooked finger of shops,
dusk falling behind their steep-pitched roofs.
Each window glazed a green-lit yellow
and framing someone at work: a calligrapher pausing
before the brushstroke, a girl bent over lace.
I hold an address folded in my pocket.

What I want is a photograph
of my dead teacher, and I've been told
that a woman on this street can create it.
When I walk in, she sits me down, smiling.
Her hands on my head this way, that.
Then into a darkroom to lift the paper from its bath.

He's sitting alone on a jetty, he's saying
something — one large hand raised slightly
in an indeterminate gesture, open grace
of the fingers tracing some missing word.
Around him a rubble of bleached rocks
and broken concrete — and the jetty is cracked:

a long, widening fissure which will island him
eventually, separate him from all the junk
piled up on the other side — bottle glass
and tires, rusted bedsprings, tin cans.
The print already going coppery at the edges, fading.
I tell her this is exactly the photograph

I had in mind. Then step outside — the picture
gone to negative now, the street deadending
into saltgrass. After the news came, I kept seeing
the road in his poem disappearing —

his car stalled, the silence filling it like water,
shoring itself up against the worn stone of his voice:

I wasn't afraid, I should have been afraid.
And: *I could hear time cease, the field quietly widen.*

River

for Larry Levis

You want to tell this story
without touching anything.
The glass unsmudged, the great river
still frozen. Or if it was raining then,
the rain falling unbroken.

There are no people in this story,
no one you'd know. It's January,
March, that fine gray suspension
before the thaw. It's a long walk,
that's all, hands deep in the pockets,

rough wind of diesel and prairie,
years go by. You carry a few words
like compasses, that's all, like coins,
bright eye-pennies, their cool weight
precise in the palms.

Praying with George Herbert in Late Winter

1

In fits and starts, Lord,
   our words work
the other side of language

where you lie if you can be said
   to lie. Mercy upon
the priest who calls on you

to nurture and to terrorize
   him, for you oblige.
Mercy upon you, breath's engine

returning what is to what is.
   Outside, light swarms
and particularizes the snow;

tree limbs crack with ice
   and drop. I can say
there is a larger something

inside me. I can say,
   "Gratitude is
a strange country." But what

would I give to live there?

2

     Something breaks in us,
and keeps breaking. Charity,

be severe with me.
Mercy, lay on your hands.

White robes on
the cypress tree. Sparrows
            clot the fence posts;
they hop once and weave

through the bleached air.
Lord, I drift on the words
            I speak to you —
the words take on

and utter me. In what
language are you not
            what *we* say you are?
Surprise me, Lord, as a seed

surprises itself . . .

3
    Today the sun has the inward look
of the eye of the Christ Child.
    Grace falls at odd angles from heaven

    to earth: my sins are bright sparks
in the dark of blamelessness . . .
    Yes. From my window I watch a boy step

    backwards down the snow-covered road,
studying his sudden boot tracks.
    The wedding of his look and the world!

    And for a moment, Lord, I think
I understand about you and silence . . .
    But what a racket I make in telling you.

Reading Frank O'Hara in the Hospital

1

The IV drips its slow news.
So long, lean and turbulent morning!
I wonder if my roommate would swap

2

Schlegel's *Lucinde* for his scrambled eggs?
Each thing bears its gifts,
the power lines' birds settle and cry out:

3

"You too could be Premier of France,
if only . . .
if only . . . "

4

The lights
in here are so excitement prone!
but the sun is undefended. Doctor,

5

I feel like I'm rushing
toward you with an olive branch . . .
With my cheese sandwich and wrist tag,

6

I could be six years old again —
look out, jungle gym! Now
outside I hear "a bulldozer in heat

7

stuck in mud." And the world
narrows to this window above
the hospital gift shop. No, it widens.

Evening Song

The crickets go on with their shrill music.
The sun drops down.

What was it my brother said to me once
in Charleston, before he disappeared that spring
like the quick wake of a water mite?

This was 1980, evening, the porch lights burning.
He was reading from *The Cloud of Unknowing.*

Robins gossiped in the poplars,
moths spiraled across the uncut grass.
Moonlight wormed through the neighboring lawns.

We must therefore pray . . . not in many words,
but in a little word of one syllable.

Didn't he say forgiveness was his homely double?
Didn't he say what I wanted him to say? Maybe
I wasn't listening, chewing a branch of sassafras . . .

But I doubt it. As I doubt, now, that the life
of my lawn is a still life, the moon and shrill chants

opinions on despair. There are times
when the sound the world makes is a little word.
Something like *help*, or *yes* . . .

Benton's Clouds

The background is clouds and clouds above those
the color of an exhaustion, whether
of field hands stacking sheaves, or the coiling,
columnar exhaust of a coal engine.

It is eighteen seventy in nineteen
twenty-seven in nineteen ninety-eight.
The colors of his clouds express each new
or brooding effluence felt elsewhere as

progress, no matter which foreground story,
no matter the gandy dancer contoured
as corn field, no matter Persephone
naked as herself, as a sinew of

rock ledge or oak root yet pornographic
under the modern elder leering down.
The background is everywhere telling.
In the present moment, in the real air,

what we saw above the lake was an art —
gulls and then no gulls, swirl of vacation
debris twirling in funnels from the pier
though the wind rushed in wilder off the surge,

clouds, then not clouds but a green-gray progress
of violences in the lowing air, waves

like a bad blow under water. We stood
at the pier railing and watched it come on.

It is too late to behold the future,
if by future what we mean is the passed-
over detail in the painting which tells
where the scene is destined to lead — Benton's

brilliance, beside the roiling billowy
cloud banks blackened as battlefield debris,
beside the shapely physique of nature
on the move, its machinery of change,

is history in an instant. How else
infuse his Reconstruction pastorals,
his dreamy midwifes, sod farmers, dancing
hay bales wrapped in billows of sallow light,

with an agony befitting the some-
time expatriate Modernist Wobbly
harmonica player he was. Who else
could execute such a beautiful storm,

whipped white, first a color on the water
like a wing or natural improvement.
When the Coast Guard boat swept by us waving,
it was already too late and too close.

The storm took down the big tree in seconds.
Though we were running, swirl of muscle, bales
and billows of fear like the wind breaking
over each swell with the force of a hand,

though we cleared the first breakwall and elm grove,
it was only accident the baby's
carriage was not crushed by the linden bough
sheared off, clean as old bone. We were standing

. . .

in the grinding rain, too soon still for tears —
it was too soon to tell what damages
there would be, though we knew, as in his art,
as though before the last skier had tipped

into the lake, there was peril ahead.
We could see it all in an instant's clear
likeness, where the future is not coming
but is already part of the story.

Ohio Fields after Rain

The slow humped backs of ice ceased
to shadow the savannahs of Ohio millennia
ago, right where we've sailed to a stop.
The shaken woman leaves open her car door
and familiar as relatives we touch hands
in the middle of the wet, black road.
To the north new corn enriches by the hour.

South of us — really, just over a fence —
heavy boulders rolled thousands of miles
quit the migration and grew down,
huddled, cropped, scarred by the journey.
"I couldn't," she says, "stop skidding,"
and I know what she means, having
felt the weight of my car planing a scant

millimeter over the highway glaze. Calmly
she slid to one shoulder, I to the other,
and the earth spun onward without us.
What a place we have come to, scooped
hollow of hillsides, cut valleys, drumlins
and plains. And where the rain settles,
the gray beasts growing tame on the shore.

Treatise on Touch

Whom to believe? This is our central task.
My love lies pierced in the throat by needles.
She holds still as a branch on the white cot — .
It is a matter of training, of touch,

as the doctor probes the nerve ganglia
in the base of her neck. He pushes blind
with the tip of a needle to deaden
each nerve to her hurt hands without numbing

her eyes, her auditor channels, her heart,
or any other system wrapped a thin
thread away against the ladder of spine.
The worried nurse keeps talking aerobics

as she cocks her syringe of medicine —
when he whispers *aspirate*, quickly she
draws it into a clear tube like good air.
Inject and she presses, she shoots it in.

To the eye the grounds are custodial,
every shrub, rose, cluster of trees clipped
or shorn in devoted form, so children
see discipline as an order of care.

The pathway through the green, medieval yards
is the same, to church or to class, and lined
like cathedral rooftops with witnesses,
gargoyles in stoneworks, stations of the cross,

the melancholy watchers of the faith,
and the Sisters of Divine Providence
laid to rest in the nunnery graveyard
only steps off the path. To visit them

• • •

daily is a march the parochial
children dread. And when she brings me to see,
two decades since, I feel the remnant fear
in the way she holds herself, and anger,

the way the woman I love is a child
again watched by the watchers from above.
It is a game to kiss the air, whisper's-
breath over the lips, though the nuns waiting

whose sister lies still in her coffin think
the children will learn to love or fear their
own lives better, blessing the mouth of the
dead. Whom to believe? To the touch the grounds

are fertile, fruitful with pain, the needling
undergrowth, dense pollen brushed at the nose,
the figure of the martyr hung and pierced,
a hand struck in punishment from pure air . . .

Divine I am inside and out, and I
make holy whatever I touch or am
touched from . . . To touch my person to someone
else's is about as much as I can stand.

Now the nurse holds her hand steady to clear
the path the medicine takes through the tube.
They don't really know what is wrong. The weeks
have brought only pain, how the slightest touch

burns from the fingertips upward, wrists, fore-
arms, elbows, until even the muscle
mass, the tissue, atrophies. She cannot
hold a spoon or brush our child's hair to sleep.

She cannot hold her body still to sleep.
A doctor tells her, use them or they'll fail —

another thinks it best to wait and gives
her medicine though it makes her bleed,

as if miscarrying, pregnant from a
lover's touch she only dreamed she may have
known. Whom to believe? *The rays that come from
heavenly worlds will separate between*

him and what he touched. — The doctors don't agree.
There I feel that nothing can befall me
in life, — no disgrace, no calamity
(leaving me my eyes), which nature cannot

repair. Therefore,
                    I believe my love, who
lies still as a stone below her good nurse.
I believe the children walking the path,
watching the bees, and the bells which call them

to music or mass, immaculate song.
I believe this pain, which makes us all sing —
the song like a finger pointing down, damned,
and the eyes of the faithful gazing back.

Bad Cello

My bad cello! I love it
too much, my note to almost note,
my almost Bach, my almost Haydn, two who
heard things falling off a shelf —
they never thought that
was music. Try wind
at night, one whispers. Try that
against your good night's
sleep. Still, something's passing, same
as grief — there's no
word for it. Same as joy
but only in the flourish of up and down, the way
a note is held — or held off —
too long.
        Certain afternoons are
private, forsythia against the window,
its hundreds of branches I should have
cut in summer, their
scratch-scratch-scratchity. So I practice
to them, so I practice
with them.
        I keep thinking
how Brahms slept right through
my childhood, that print in a frame
above my grandmother's threadbare couch, and how
I loved his face completely. His eyes
were closed. He leaned against the piano.
And above him all those
other faces — Beethoven and Bach and Mozart —
misty currents they floated in said *dream*, said

go away, Brahms is having a vision right now,
said *Brahms needs his nap.*

                                It's just that — bad cello! —
the rondo? I like it, like to play it twice because
no words! Because *I do it*
so badly! Delicious part
going minor, right
down the hole, neither-what-I-thought-nor-
what-I-dreamt. Dark in there. Strange.

I Imagine the Mortician

I imagine a mortician looks at the hands
first, the lines up toward the fingers,
then down toward the fleshy parts, how
one crevice crosses at an angle
and stops. I imagine this on a summer day.
Or I imagine myself walking early morning,
really early, when it's still half dark,
imagining with each step that poor
mortician in some cool room across town
faced with a slug of a thing — no one
he knows — merely weight now. Or perhaps
I *was* walking, but the thought
stopped me. I didn't dare
look at my hand, its own
scattered lines, webs that go nowhere.
But the mortician? Probably
a bored one too, one who half-hates
his job, whose father and grandfather
made him, he had no choice, not really,
though the hands — they are
interesting, aren't they? It might be
a hobby of his that perks up the whole
awful business, gauging the lifeline
against the real life, watching the years

stop short, then bringing the body
back to the world in his dream
of that body, flashing it back to the yard,
bright sun, garden shears, blackberries.
I walked this morning — that's
the truth of it. How was I to know? The air
only gradually gave up its dark. My mind —
only birdsong entered, sound
like pebbles tied together with string
and trailing off. So I let
the mortician in
with his bent curiosity, the reverse
of the new mother who counts
all the toes and fingers
and is so relieved.

Bones Not of This Puny World

Those saints, the ones
who sat high on poles, and looked down
half dizzy or with their eyes
shut, I think
about them, not constantly, just
occasionally, how seen from below,
they were wiry
bent shapes, which meant they were
praying, repeating some
fabulous, modest sentence — *forgive me,*
mother of all things that walk
or swim or fly, that think
or refuse to think — or they were
simply glazed over, going
lockjawed into that
holy blank. It was hot
in those places. People came in crowds
to look up, to exhort or to praise

or just to be part of the hardest
of landscapes, rocks
and scrawny trees, because those poles
were it, the center of life, like the quiet
blue-green iris can take
over the eye and float there and make it
famous. But what hopeless amoeba
is the mind after 35 years
on a pole, the sun past
blinding, *modesty forbids me* — past that,
because you've chucked
the clothes, you've
chucked the bits of childhood you might
have cherished, you've chucked
the walking around, talking to this one,
to that one, you've chucked
chucking anything so it's all
a vague blob you might, *might,*
nod to and then happily dream of, i.e.:
forget. Daniel the Stylite
(409–493), they had to break
his body when they finally figured out
he'd been dead three days. He came apart
too easily, like the old tinkertoys
my brother loved, small clicks at the joints
as they piled up bone and flesh,
reverently folding the cloth around it,
tying it with something — strips of leather,
or maybe they had rope by then.
Maybe they had a lot of things
by then: carts, and a few
hand-lettered books, emptiness
and anger, sadness for sure — *poor*
poor slob — or even irony
which lives in sadness
as a wing lives in certain insects
that can't fly but have
powerful legs whose needles flash.

And sharp like that, such irony —
sure, baked by God himself. No,
nobody talked like that — most of them
scared witless handling
the bones-not-of-this-puny-world.
And the monks' lamentation? My *Oxford Book
of Saints* says it was like "a clap
of thunder." But thunder follows
lightning and grows huge
on sudden air. And when the human weight
comes down? Wasn't there one guy
shaking his head
the way we walk around, shaking
our heads at every earnest foolishness,
people crazy the world
is ending on March 25th, say, who give away
their clothes and their cars, their
only good TV? I imagine
being Daniel sometimes. Past hunger
like that, past thirst, past
the sweetness of all that
giving up, how thin the body
can be, like paper one holds
to the light, and one's wish to be anything
even thinner than that.
What is desire anyway? A ribbon. A leaf.
A mechanical pencil. I *think*
about Daniel. How he looked down
from his altitude and saw people sometimes
looking up, looking — what? — amazed
or indifferent, or after a while
yawning, going off to wherever
people always go. Then there was
nothing down there in the dark but the road,
and mostly no road, just the tired expanse
of desert, no line between earth
and not-earth. Some nights, such stars
came out that he looked up, but not

to love them. I think about that —
not to love them — and the sky goes
brilliant in bits that drift
nowhere, and are steady,
and give no sign.

Lament

At Safeway, on ice, the octopus —
great bulbous purple head
folded over, arms too many
and haphazard, pulled up like someone needed
to sweep the gleaming case *right now*.
Among tidy shrimp
and yawning tuna, it's the sideshow
freak, a thing
stopped and falling through
everything it was, past
strange to terrible to odd, dim star
between sun and moon though
the sky's all wrong, neither
day or night,
this cool fluorescence.

How old is he? I ask the kid
behind the counter, who shrugs, who
half-smiles. I look for the eye buried
in the blue-green folds. So many
eons in there. So many years
life shifting color turned to charm
the eternal underwater where it might
be asleep like that, or simply pretending —
awful eerie sea life morgue . . .

But what if I claimed
the body? What if I took it and kept

walking, crossing the dismal
parking lot, its weight against me, dear
tangle of arms in its
paper shroud. What if I stood then
and fumbled with the keys, and gave it
to the darkness
filling the old back seat.
And blessed it twice, the second time
too long and endless
as water. What then —
And who would I be. And where
would I drive.

from *dreampoems*

dreampoem 3

the actual leads inward
to a street somewhere unknown to me
lit as though by amber.

that is: a false cinematic glow encompassed all I passed by
& I was not taken in.

Beautiful man! I shouted & my voice then
traveled, my voice lifted out of itself —

I heard my own voice
cold against the cobbles, hot against the cobbles
& the street's shine grew flashy —

but this was in my mind.

the actual leads inwards & I was with
the sodden hills, the drenched tree limbs,
the cave shadows.

I want you to understand

I am who I was then, my hair in my eyes

it was dark & the mountains were memories

dreampoem 4

now they lift over the groomed trees,
the birds.
the white sky.
spire. peak.
the way is flight
always the way, away.

if this sentiment offends you be assured my heart is not in it.
& the doomed flight may undo itself
once there, wherever,
        in the variable day.

so many objects, though, so much
accounting for: bicycles, jackets, bees —
the smoked glass over the eye
uncovers the street's miraculous blur,
vaguely brazen.

don't come much closer.
the landscape is breathing beautifully its entire beauty.
& the groomed trees are filled with lungs
& the stationary stone carved columns are not dying, even.

all in all, the world is not real enough.

dreampoem 6

envision this night:
gray brood
gray nuzzle against stone

I should be happier —

• • •

the anxious light beneath
the panicked moon

sky full of egret
(regret)
screeching at 7 pm

as song by song we loosen
round vaults in us —

a rule of sky
like the stars' non-existence —

a rule of heart
proclaiming hapless routes

so no nothing, no steering toward or away

& words parade in stiff tongues
Dante's stiffs soaking up the light

bravely wallowing

swan song swallow song

dreampoem 7

from fire
Heraclitus deduced
the world's hot core

growing complicated.
In as much as time is motion,
is fickle-hearted, is totally irrational —

• • •

say
not eternal.
& mean it.

so what is there,
after all this fucking
but more fucking

that we may douse
whatever flickers in us
wind-blown so that our

tongues melt
even as they flame.

excuse me.

these days
deep in an odd winter
amid certain unreasonable chimes

in the slant of a certain, amazed light
I figure things differently.

dreampoem 8

I was not amazed by anything.
I stung myself.
I beatified myself.
& the planets were swooning
in their small, unratified oval lights

. . .

like stillness
& unlike stillness
& the cups & saucers no longer rattled.
& the sheets remained as were

implacably creased
with deep purple astonished shadows
& yellow peaks.

beyond the window
above the concrete ledge
we saw some blue of sky
angular & tossed.

that was when the future glanced back at us

dreampoem 10

there are things in this world impossible to calculate
though we persist
believing
it will be all beautiful in the end
in the end surely beauty awaits

not so

the world goes on without us
idling her spare gears
whittling

her doomed edges
& the cloudy, deceptive smile
which graced us just seconds ago

. . .

has its correlative
but not its twin.
I am here of my own accord

nonetheless —
lipsticked, vacuous
the ideal world is never far from us

from our conceptions of it
like the cells' destiny
careening

toward death & pleasure at the same time.

I am wearing a blue shirt.

I am forgetting all about you.

from "The Truth about God: Seventeen Poems"

My Religion

My religion makes no sense
and does not help me
therefore I pursue it.

When we see
how simple it would have been
we will thrash ourselves.

I had a vision
of all the people in the world
who are searching for God

massed in a room
on one side
of a partition

that looks
from the other side
(God's side)

transparent
but we are blind.
Our gestures are blind.

Our blind gestures continue
for some time until finally
from somewhere

. . .

on the other side of the partition there we are
looking back at them.
It is far too late.

We see how brokenly
how warily
how ill

our blind gestures
parodied
what God really wanted

(some simple thing).
The thought of it
(this simple thing)

is like a creature
let loose in a room
and battering

to get out.
It batters my soul
with its rifle butt.

Flexion of God

I have a friend who is red hot with pain.
He feels the lights like hard rain through his pores.
Together we went to ask Isaac.

Isaac said I will tell you the story told to me.
It was from Adam
issued the lights.

. . .

From the lights of his forehead were formed all the names of the world.
From the lights of his ears, nose and throat
came a function no one has ever defined.

From the lights of his eyes — but wait —
Isaac waits.
In theory

the lights of the eye should have issued from Adam's navel.
But within the lights themselves occurred
an intake of breath

and they changed their path.
And they were separated.
And they were caught in the head.

And from these separated lights came
what pains you
on its errands (here my friend began to weep) through the world.

For be assured it is not only you who mourn.
Isaac lashed his tail.
Every rank of world

was caused to descend
(at least one rank)
by the terrible pressure of the light.

Nothing remained in place.
Nothing was not captured except
among the shards and roots and matter

some lights
from Adam's eyes
nourished there somehow.

• • •

Isaac stopped his roaring.
And my friend by now drowsy as a snake subsided
behind a heap of blueblack syllables.

God's Name

God had no name.
Isaac had two names.
Isaac was also called The Blind.

Inside the dark sky of his mind
Isaac could hear God
moving down a country road bordered by trees.

By the way the trees reflected off God
Isaac knew which ones were straight and tall
or when they carried their branches

as a body does its head
or why some crouched low to the ground in thickets.
To hear how God was moving through the universe

gave Isaac his question.
I could tell you his answer
but it wouldn't help.

The name is not a noun.
It is an adverb.
Like the little black notebooks that Beethoven carried

in his coatpocket
for the use of those who wished to converse with him,
the God adverb

. . .

is a one-way street that goes everywhere you are.
No use telling you what it is.
Just chew it and rub it on.

The Wolf God

Like a painting we will be erased, no one can remain.
I saw my life as a wolf loping along the road
and I questioned the women of that place.

Some regard the wolf as immortal, they said.
Now you know this only happened in one case and that
wolves die regularly of various causes —

bears kill them, tigers hunt them,
they get epilepsy,
they get a salmon bone crosswise in their throat,

they run themselves to death no one knows why —
but perhaps you never heard
of their ear trouble.

They have very good ears,
can hear a cloud pass overhead.
And sometimes it happens

that a windblown seed will bury itself in the aural canal
displacing equilibrium.
They go mad trying to stand upright,

nothing to link with.
Die of anger.
Only one we know learned to go along with it.

. . .

He took small steps at first,
using the updrafts.
They called him Huizkol,

that means
Looks Good in Spring.
Things are as hard as you make them.

God's Ardor

mit meinem Seufzer in das Feuer

God has been given a tape of Lucifer's from hell.
God was nervous all day
and put off listening to it.

Who am I to say but they are parallel characters,
under stress.
Listening to the tape

God fell forward on his knees
with one arm flat against the ground.
God turned blue with cold.

Then took the form of a cup of water.
Then a hunter scorching his horn.
Then slumber.

Motionless God fell and fell and fell.
Angels flowed up through His intellect by the thousands
then they were gone.

For the rest of the night
God sat like a wife watching the slow fields
enter and release their illegible white sighs.

Argos

If you think Odysseus too strong and brave to cry,
that the god-loved, god-protected hero
when he returned to Ithaka disguised,
intent to check up on his wife

and candidly apprise the condition of his kingdom
so that he steeled himself resolutely against surprise
and came into his land cold-hearted, clear-eyed,
ready for revenge, then you read Homer as I did,

too fast, knowing you'd be tested for plot
and major happenings, skimming forward to the massacre,
the shambles engineered with Telémakhos
by turning beggar and taking up the challenge of the bow.

Reading this way you probably missed the tear
Odysseus shed for his decrepit dog, Argos,
who's nothing but a bag of bones asleep atop
a refuse pile outside the palace gates. The dog is not

a god in earthly clothes, but in its own disguise
of death and destitution is more like Ithaka itself.
And if you returned home after twenty years
you might weep for the hunting dog

you long ago abandoned, rising from the garbage
of its bed, its instinct of recognition still intact,
enough will to wag its tail, lift its head, but little more.
Years ago you had the chance to read that page more closely

. . .

but instead you raced ahead, like Odysseus, cocksure
with your plan. Now the past is what you study,
where guile and speed give over to grief so you might stop,
and desiring to weep, weep more deeply.

Brave Sparrow

whose home is in the straw
and baling twine threaded
in the slots of a roof vent

who guards a tiny ledge
against the starlings
that cruise the neighborhood

whose heart is smaller
than a heart should be,
whose feathers stiffen

like an arrow fret to quicken
the hydraulics of its wings,
stay there on the metal

ledge, widen your alarming
beak, but do not flee as others have
to the black walnut vaulting

overhead. Do not move outside
the world you've made
from baling twine and straw.

The isolated starling fears
the crows, the crows gang up
to rout a hawk. The hawk

. . .

is cold. And cold is what
a larger heart maintains.
The owl at dusk and dawn,

far off, unseen, but audible,
repeats its syncopated intervals,
a song that's not a cry

but a whisper rising from concentric
rings of water spreading out across
the surface of a catchment pond.

It asks, "Who are you? Who
are you?" but no one knows.
Stay where you are, nervous, jittery.

Move your small head a hundred
ways, a hundred times, keep
paying attention to the terrifying

world. And if you see the robins
in their dirty orange vests
patrolling the yard like thugs,

forget about the worm. Starve
yourself, or from the air inhale
the water you may need, digest

the dust. And what the promiscuous
cat and jaybirds do, let them
do it, let them dart and snipe,

let them sound like others.
They sleep when the owl sends
out its encircling question.

Stay where you are, you lit fuse,
you dull spark of saltpeter and sulfur.

My Crucifixion

Not blasphemy so much as curiosity
and imitation suggested I lie face up
and naked on my bedroom floor,
arms stretched out like His,

feet crossed at the ankles,
and my head lolling in that familiar
defeated way, while my sisters worked
with toy wooden hammers to drive

imagined spikes through my hands and feet.
A spiritual exercise? I don't think so.
For unlike Christ my boy-size penis stiffened
like one of Satan's fingers.

I was dying a savior's death and yet
what my sisters called my "thing,"
struggled against extinction
as if its resurrection could not be held off

by this playful holy torture, nor stopped
except by the arrival of my parents,
who stood above us suddenly like prelates,
home early from their supper club,

stunned, but not astonished, to find
the babysitter asleep and the inquisitive
nature of our heathenish hearts amok
in murderous pageantry.

The Barber

Even in death he roams the yard in his boxer shorts,
plowing the push-mower through bermuda grass,
bullying it against the fence and tree trunks,
chipping its twisted blades on the patio's edge.

The chalky flint and orange spark of struck concrete
floats in the air, tastes like metal, smells
like the slow burn of hair on his electric clippers.
And smelling it, I feel the hot shoe of the shaver

as he guided it in a high arc around my ears,
then set the sharp toothy edge against my sideburns
to trim them square, and how he used his huge stomach
to butt the chair and his flat hand palming my head

to keep me still, pressing my chin down as he cleaned
the ragged wisps of hair along my neck.
A fat inconsolable man whose skill and pleasure
was to clip and shear, to make raw and stubble

all that grew in this world, expose the scalp,
the place of roots and nerves and make vulnerable,
there in the double mirrors of his shop, the long
stem-muscles of our necks. And so we hung below

his license in its cheap black frame, above the violet
light of the scissors shed with its glass jars
of germicide and the long tapered combs soaking
in its blue iridescence. Gruff when he wasn't silent,

he was a neighbor to fear, yet we trusted him
beyond his anger, beyond his privacy. He was like a father
we could hate, a foil for our unspent vengeance,
though vengeance was always his. He sent us back

. . .

into the world burning and itching, alive with the horror
of closing eyes in the pinkish darkness
of his shop and having felt the horse-hair brush, talc-filled,
cloying, too sweet for boyhood, whisked across the face.

Bardo

... dark wide realm where we walk
with everyone.
— Thom Gunn

Dangerously frail is what his hand was like
when he showed up at our house,
three or four days after his death
and stood at the foot of our bed.

Though we had expected him to appear
in some form, it was odd, the clarity
and precise decrepitude of his condition,
and how his hand, frail as it was,

lifted me from behind my head, up from the pillow,
so that no longer could I claim it was a dream,
nor deny that what your father wanted,
even with you sleeping next to me,

was to kiss me on the lips.
There was no refusing his anointing me
with what I was meant to bear of him
from where he was, present in the world,

a document loose from the archives
of form — not spectral, not corporeal —
in transit, though not between lives or bodies:
those lips on mine, then mine on yours.

The Other

When you come to the other side
of lust the body lays itself
down in others as itself
no longer and the fields till now
fallow, bloom, vermilion.

When you cross to the other side
of pride the heart withers
into tinder, the wind blesses it.
Your body flares, white sticks
this side of anger.

Arriving at the other side
of terror, the voice is a dark flame
walking evenings in the garden,
your name unknown to it
if the last light calls you.

And when you have passed the other side
of hope the shore will blaze
finally. We are all light here.
Do not look for me or ask.
You will never have known me.

Final Season

Outside this nursing home I'm not helpless
but here I am, come to visit them, my mother

ninety, almost blind, almost deaf, my father
just slightly better, both in wheelchairs.
Their lives are now completely routine.
Beyond the sealed windows rolls on some season.

Before my visit here I knew the season.
But now, come to live among the helpless
I'm nowhere, stripped of my routine.
Today I am a mother to my mother.
I move the spoon to her tongue above the wheelchair.
All I see is her tongue, then I see my father's

approaching to be fed by me, the father,
time out of focus in this kind of season,
moments become months like spokes of a wheelchair
turning too slowly for me to see them, helpless,
lifting the eighty-five pounds become my mother
to her bed. These are my days, hobbled to their routine.

Bedtime and rising: the worst of our routine.
First there is the preparation of my father,
then the long resistance of my mother
who would not have me see her naked this season
of her life when she is every day more helpless.
Her mind, off-center, careens, a racing wheelchair

but keeping its own pattern like her wheelchair
on which she can depend to continue her routine,
wheeling to the bathroom, the dining room, not helpless
in her own eyes, *Not like him,* she shouts out at father
though together they move the same velocity this season
and shouting at anyone is not how I remember Mother.

I close my eyes this morning: suddenly she is Mommie
gripping my hand at the Detroit Zoo (not a wheelchair
housing a stranger slapping my wrist this season
when I hand her coffee in my routine

of waking them up), my other hand in Daddy's
swinging me up — I'm three — to stare down on the crocodile, helpless.

I have no age at all, without a wheelchair in this routine
with a mother not a mother in her final season,
helpless, not a child or man, without a father.

Nocturne with Witch, Oven and Two Little Figures

Haphazardly a blizzard collects over our window
as if the moon, weaving between clouds, were breathing it.

In the same window seat, stitched with lilies, each minute prickly,
in which she read me fifty-five years back

her favorite, "Hansel and Gretel,"
I am reading to my sister the same tale tonight.

She is sixty-eight, I am fifty-eight.
Now when she fidgets, as if from inattention,

I slam *The Brothers Grimm* down on her head
just as she slammed me at three, spitting a word

like a black worm I spit back at her. I shake her, screaming
if she dares to cry or tell our mother or father

I will come into her room at midnight
as I did last night dressed as The Boogie Man,

a pair of scissors in my hand to cut her weenie off.
But I don't have one, stupid, she laughs, shrilly

. . .

and it is her voice from age thirteen, a voice-over
of her voice now, post-menopausal, grating over it.

Here the book cracks open, we step into it,
the wood stretches before us, gnarled, primeval

and we are hand in hand as our real parents planned
we should be in their version of the tale

where brother and sister adventure with a good witch,
something like the old maid fifth grade teacher

my sister and I shared, dwarfed, hunchbacked,
always in black and chalk-enshrouded

because she crashed erasers together like cymbals, grinning
while she crashed unceasingly, beaming, scolding a class,

or if there were a bad witch for them she was a teacher
of moral precept stiff and upright as the paddling sticks

I suffered, just like my sister, a stiff dose of weekly
at Bushnell Congregational Sunday School.

Now as the dream continues, I shrink, sprout wings
until I am a tiny raven, I fly atop a tree.

My sister trundles on, happy without me, toward the witch's house,
little aware that what awaits her, ravenous, magical

is a shadow of herself, spectral in the doorway
and after she sates herself with delicious architecture

she will enter in to be devoured by herself,
witch and sister one in the pot brought to a boil

in this, the other life, where I am author.

My Crow, Your Crow

Crow light: I call it that at dawn
when one wing, then this other, bursts in flame,
catching the sun's rising. The stupid bird,
dipping his hunk of bread into the water,
doesn't know the Mississippi is my friend:
it disgorges in the gulf the frozen states I came from.
Mississippi! She was a grade school spelling word
in Detroit for me. I spelled well. Now, forty years later
I jog beside her interchange of gold and silver lustres,
always too much in love with any surface of the world.
But the crow: I know it's not the same bird
morning after morning. Still, the dipping of his beak
into this water, softening a breakfast for his gullet
demanding, like mine, daily satisfactions
lets me pretend every day's the same.
On one chunk of that bread some day up ahead
my last day is written, clear as the printing
on my birth certificate on file in Michigan.
Crows dip their bread. Daily, I run for breath,
hoping to extend my distance, even a little.
The Mississippi muddies, clears, according to the factories
up North, the local, snarled measures against its dying.
Slowly, even the river is passing from us while I run.

For Lear

I have to get this down before the light dies.
That leaves me thirteen minutes before sunset at 6:14.

A minute gone already? Here I go, the best I can:
my mother called at dawn; my father's in the hospital

again, reason unknown, and I saw my own exhaustion,
half a century's staggering toward me at noon

. . .

crazed, so the afternoon, out of time
was a kind of night, starless, cloudless, sleepless,

where I wandered, terrified and cold
though the gulf wind bearing me along New Orleans streets

tried to tell me the end will be a kind of balm
such as the drowned know, surrendering their bodies.

I have to say this: every year now
you are increasing in my life, Lear.

I see you in the old man living in the parking lot
of my bank, sleeping on money bags emptied

of the world's currencies, and the tellers appear
punching in to give him table scraps for his repasts

while the cops and street gangs hail him and pass on.
Or the other ancient one, shopping cart his home,

who wanders the highway, preaching to passing traffic,
or the legless one who begs cathedral steps all day.

These have all survived themselves. Who am I to know
if my father — if I — will be passed over

as these have been when the reaper swings through,
determined to curb the excess of our numbers, Lear,

as if some should be spared to parade a fine madness
such as I hope to display in motley, growing old

but I would not wish on my father in his mildness,
and as I, too, might imitate against my inclination

when the button will not be undone, when my time comes.

The God Who Loves You

It must be troubling for the god who loves you
To ponder how much happier you'd be today
Had you been able to glimpse your many futures.
It must be painful for him to watch you on Friday evenings
Driving home from the office, content with your week —
Three fine houses sold to deserving families —
Knowing as he does exactly what would have happened
Had you gone to your second choice for college.
Knowing the roommate you'd have been allotted
Whose ardent opinions on painting and music
Would have kindled in you a life-long passion.
A life thirty points above the life you're living
On any scale of satisfaction. And every point
A thorn in the side of the god who loves you.
You don't want that, a large-souled man like you
Who tries to withhold from your wife the day's disappointments
So she can save her empathy for the children.
And would you want this god to compare your wife
With the woman you were destined to meet on the other campus?
It hurts you to think of him ranking the conversation
You'd have enjoyed over there higher in insight
Than the conversation you're used to.
And think how this loving god would feel
Knowing that the man next in line for your wife
Would have pleased her more than you ever will
Even on your best days, when you really try.
Can you sleep at night believing a god like that
Is pacing his cloudy bedroom, harassed by alternatives
You're spared by ignorance? The difference between what is
And what could have been will remain alive for him

Even after you cease existing, after you catch a chill
Running out in the snow for the morning paper,
Losing eleven years that the god who loves you
Will feel compelled to imagine scene by scene
Unless you come to the rescue by imagining him
No wiser than you are, no god at all, only a friend
No closer than the actual friend you made at college,
The one you haven't written in months. Sit down tonight
And write him about the life you can talk about
With a claim to authority, the life you've witnessed,
Which for all you know is the life you've chosen.

A Priest of Hermes

The way up, from here to there, may be closed,
But the way down, from there to here, still open
Wide enough for a slender god like Hermes
To slip from the clouds if you give your evenings
To learning about the plants under his influence,
The winged and wingless creatures, the rocks and metals,
And practice his sacred flute or dulcimer.

No prayers. Just the effort to make his stay
So full of the comforts of home he won't forget it,
To build him a shrine he finds congenial,
Something as simple as roofed pillars
Without the darkness of an interior.

If you're lucky, he'll want to sit on the steps
Under the stars for as long as you live
And sniff the fragrance of wine and barley
As it blows from the altar on a salty sea breeze.
He'll want, when you die, to offer his services
As a guide on the shadowy path to the underworld.

. . .

Not till you reach the watery crossing
Will he leave your side, and even then
He'll shout instructions as you slip from your shoes
And wade alone into that dark river.

Not the Idle

It's not the idle who move us but the few
Often confused with the idle, those who define
Their project in life in terms so ample
Nothing they ever do is a digression.
Each episode contributes its own rare gift
As a chapter in *Moby-Dick* on squid or hard tack
Is just as important to Ishmael as a fight with a whale.
The few who refuse to live for the plot's sake,
Major or minor, but for texture and tone and hue.
For them weeding a garden all afternoon
Can't be construed as a detour from the road of life.
The road narrows to a garden path that turns
And circles to show that traveling goes only so far
As a metaphor. The day rests on the grass.
And at night the books of these few,
Lined up on their desks, don't look like drinks
Lined up on a bar to help them evade their troubles.
They look like an escort of mountain guides
Come to conduct the climber to a lofty outlook
Rising serene above the fog. For them the view
Is no digression though it won't last long
And they won't remember even the vivid details.
The supper with friends back in the village
In a dining room brightened with flowers and paintings
No digression for them though the talk leads
To no breakthrough. The topic they happen to hit on
Isn't a ferry to carry them over the interval
Between soup and salad. It's a raft drifting downstream
Where the banks widen to embrace a lake

And birds rise from the reeds in many colors.
Everyone tries to name them and fails
For an hour no one considers idle.

Gelati

These songs from the corner church,
Wafting through the window this August morning,
Lift the job of sanding my scarred oak bookcase
From a three, on a ten-point scale of joy,
To at least a four. Not a bad grade
For an enterprise mainly practical, preparing a site
Fittingly handsome for the noble shelf-load
Of Roman stoics whose sensible pages,
Stacked now on my speakers, don't register on the joy chart.
A cold wind blows from their doctrine that a virtuous life
Is in harmony with the cosmos — the cold, companionless cosmos
That never comes through when you need a friend.
No wonder the early Christians won followers.
No wonder their living descendants sound joyful still
As they proclaim that even here, near the corner
Of Hodge and Elmwood, the soul may be quickened.

These singers have had a brush with vision
Denied me so far, though once, on the Appian way,
Three miles outside of Rome, after I'd walked for hours,
Inspecting the roadside tombs, alone, in the heat of August,
Wishing I'd brought a water jug, ready to turn back,
A man pushing a cart suddenly staged an advent
As he intoned, *"Limonata, gelati,"* as if to a crowd
Though the road was empty. An old man
With a bright escutcheon of ice cream staining his apron,
Proclaiming that to ask is to have for the lucky few
Who know what to ask for.

. . .

For a minute it seemed the Bureau of Joy was calling
About a windfall blowing my way to guarantee
An eight or nine on the joy chart even if many wishes
Down on my list wouldn't be granted.
Today I seem to be focusing on my wish to sand
And stain and varnish my bookcase, a job that a monk
Who specializes in repetition might embrace as a ritual.
Let the moment expand, he says to himself,
Till time is revealed to be delusion.

For me, here in the passing hour,
The wind-borne singing brightens the moment,
However faintly it enters, however it might be improved
By the brighter acoustics of the New Jerusalem.
And now it's time for a string quartet in a new recording.
And now it's time for the baseball game on the radio.

Whether the players regard the sport as joy
Or simply as work, the crowd seems alive
With the wish to compress a lifetime
Down to a single sitting. Now for the task
Of brushing the varnish on with a steady hand
While the crowd goes wild in the bottom of the ninth
As the man on first steps off the bag, a rookie
Who'll seem a savior if he gets home.

The Moth

I

More brittle of wing
Than most flying creatures,
With twin tattoos inscribed,
On its dusty self, still
Against the window screen
In the morning light
When the house is darker
Than the exterior world
Where I of my habit
Collect the morning paper,
The porch bulb a redundant
Jewel in its copper setting,
Something to be remembered.

II

Once, turned out early
From her basement apartment
By contempt and the necessity
To feed the parking meter,
I walked too many blocks
Of the just risen city,
Where I had found a space
Between the drifts and other
Vehicles the night before.
There, beside the delivery
Entry of a large hotel
Between two planters filled
With discolored ice and leaves,

Where tulip bulbs were hidden,
A woman slept upon the grating.

III

I had been betrayed!
I saw them through her window,
The way her head tilted back
For his kiss and how her back
Arched when he felt her breasts.
I recall the vision of him:
His shoulder blades through his shirt
As he worked himself against her,
Making her eyes close in
Expressions that meant her pleasure,
And the reasons for not answering
The phone when I called earlier,
An emptiness that summoned me
To the alley where her light burned.

IV

Lying on her stomach, her woolen
Scarf covering half her face,
Stringy dark hair protruding
From the fold of her ski cap,
She clung to the bars
With finger bitten gloves,
Her lumpy body stuffed
Like a filled laundry bag
From all her layers of clothes.
She must have felt protected
In this good part of the city
As the heat rose beneath her
From the generators venting,
Though her back seemed frozen.

V

The moment the buttons opened
The drapes should have closed

The way in dreams you wake
When things start getting interesting.
From my place against the glass
I willed this go no further
And walked around the corner
And pressed the bell until
She buzzed to let me in.
He passed me on the stairs.
Our favorite wine was open,
The bed itself unstraightened.
A shadow, I lay down
In the light where he had been.

Crooked Wood

Here in the brighter yard, cleared of brittle
And split branches, I tend my patch of lawn,
Inscribed sharply now by the trees' calligraphy,
The linear and curlicued, altered suggestion
Of the root work under the soil, the ropes
And threads that tie the yard together, a binding
Contract of earth and wood, my little piece
Of what was forest, wilder now below the surface

As yet unpaved. Although I love this place,
Chair in full sun in the morning, the long
Light at the end of the day that in December
Keeps my legs in shorts, my arms in short sleeves,
It's sidewalks up north I miss, their constant
Human message, the sharp heel sounds
On hurried people, the flat stamp of work
Boots on just cleared pavement, by the snowbank

Steam rising from the coffee and exhalations
Of workers on break around a manhole cover,
The abbreviated utilities scribbled in dig safe.

And what of that remembered anticipation
Going in a shop or bar, the temporary, important
Moment before the choice of an aisle or chair
When all eyes for an instant are upon you,
When your eyes seek out no match or mirror

But the oblivion of an object found, the ringing
Of the register. It's true I slept later then.
(Why does one wake early with nothing to do?)
And sometimes with my arms around someone
I proposed breakfast to her outside the apartment —
For nothing we wanted could be made of out-of-date
Milk, collected mustards, and take-out containers
From the Indian, Thai, and Chinese restaurants

Cohabiting the chill of my undefrosted refrigerator.
Hand in hand we walked to our heaven,
The greasy spoon down the block where other
Couples also dressed in last night's clothes.
Who were we then? A couple of warm ones
Under some blankets, two piles of black clothes
On a hardwood floor. Those plaster walls
Of the brownstones would not need mending.

Word comes south of a friend's death
By natural causes, meaning no one can say
What it is that so exactly fails us,
Heart or head or the veins of circulation.
I recall the crisp angles his shirt made,
His arms expressively bent through the vest
As he leaned forward to grab his whisky glass
And laughed too loudly whatever the joke.

In my trees Jeff and Jon from Crooked Wood
Have trimmed the post oak and the maple
Then hauled the truckloads to the country
Where their friends will gather around a bonfire
Of kindling branches and lengths of seasoned trunks.

A father of young children and a son of old ways,
I knock the wood of the trees in my yard that stand
Like coatless men in the simplest of drawings.

For George V. Higgins

How to Like It

These are the first days of fall. The wind
at evening smells of roads still to be traveled,
while the sound of leaves blowing across the lawns
is like an unsettled feeling in the blood,
the desire to get in a car and just keep driving.
A man and a dog descend their front steps.
The dog says, Let's go downtown and get crazy drunk.
Let's tip over all the trashcans we can find.
This is how dogs deal with the prospect of change.
But in his sense of the season, the man is struck
by the oppressiveness of his past, how his memories
which were shifting and fluid have grown more solid
until it seems he can see remembered faces
caught up among the dark places in the trees.
The dog says, Let's pick up some girls and just
rip off their clothes. Let's dig holes everywhere.
Above his house, the man notices wisps of cloud
crossing the face of the moon. Like in a movie,
he says to himself, a movie about a person
leaving on a journey. He looks down the street
to the hills outside of town and finds the cut
where the road heads north. He thinks of driving
on that road and the dusty smell of the car
heater, which hasn't been used since last winter.
The dog says, Let's go down to the diner and sniff
people's legs. Let's stuff ourselves on burgers.
In the man's mind, the road is empty and dark.
Pine trees press down to the edge of the shoulder,
where the eyes of animals, fixed in his headlights,
shine like small cautions against the night.

Sometimes a passing truck makes his whole car shake.
The dog says, Let's go to sleep. Let's lie down
by the fire and put our tails over our noses.
But the man wants to drive all night, crossing
one state line after another, and never stop
until the sun creeps into his rearview mirror.
Then he'll pull over and rest awhile before
starting again, and at dusk he'll crest a hill
and there, filling a valley, will be the lights
of a city entirely new to him.
But the dog says, Let's just go back inside.
Let's not do anything tonight. So they
walk back up the sidewalk to the front steps.
How is it possible to want so many things
and still want nothing? The man wants to sleep
and wants to hit his head again and again
against a wall. Why is it all so difficult?
But the dog says, Let's go make a sandwich.
Let's make the tallest sandwich anyone's ever seen.
And that's what they do and that's where the man's
wife finds him, staring into the refrigerator
as if into the place where the answers are kept —
the ones telling why you get up in the morning
and how it is possible to sleep at night,
answers to what comes next and how to like it.

His Favorite Blue Cup

Over the years — and Heart has had many years —
numerous objects have slipped from his possession,
some were lost, some fell apart, some got stolen.
That cowboy doll he loved as a child,
does a piece of it still remain? And the pen
he's been looking for all week, where does it hide?
His favorite blue cup which the dog broke,
the green linen shirt that at last wore out,

the Chevy convertible that wound up in the junkyard —
Heart has come to think that all these objects are together
along with absent friends, departed family members,
and pets that have traveled over to the great beyond.
Somewhere, he believes, there's a place made up
of previous houses, former gardens, and furnished
with the vanished furniture his hands have touched.
There missing friends recline on once-loved chairs.
A cat gone for twenty years naps beneath a burning lamp.
Lost clothes fill the closets, lost books line the shelves.
The trees in front, cars in back: Heart would know them all.
These days Heart's mind sometimes wanders.
He's in a daze, he's drifted off or gathering wool,
and he thinks at such times he, too, has disappeared,
that he's rambling through his composite house,
sipping coffee from his blue cup, tossing a ball
for a mutt he owned when he was six, or walking
arm and arm with a friend not seen for a dozen years.
You look pale, the friend says, you've gotten thinner.
I've been away, says Heart, I've been away.

How It Was at the End

The box was set in a hole in the ground,
a white cardboard box big enough
for a corsage, in a hole big enough for a rose bush.
It was raining; a few prayers were said.
And his granddaughter said, How did they make him so little
to put him in such a little box?
And her cousin said, How do you mean, they burned him?
A few people sprinkled dirt over the box,
but an hour later it was still uncovered,
growing sodden as the hole filled with water.
My wife showed it to me, then went to look for a shovel.
But there was no shovel, no trowel or big spoon.
We scooped up the mud with our hands

and piled it onto the white cardboard, just enough
to cover it. Then we wiped our hands on the grass —
thick, gloppy, turd-colored, mud-smelling mud —
rubbing hard. But still we found it stuck between
our fingers or under the nails, flecks of dirt
which we picked at throughout the long afternoon.
That was three days ago and the rain keeps falling.
It is October. The leaves make their bright passage
from the trees to that nothingness called eternal.

(His life was the practice)

His life was the practice of forming a single sentence which, as he grew older,
he tried to simplify, reduce its compound-complex structure into one state-
ment ruled by the separate, inviolate pronoun within which he attempted to
live, always engaged in revision and the act of becoming; as the distilled state-
ment gradually became a fleeting inquiry, a mild interrogative, which he re-
peated and refined, making it increasingly concise, almost, at his conclusion,
producing no more than a distinct sound, not quite a word, less than a cry,
which his death erased leaving the question mark hanging in the air, like a
broken halo, emblem of his birth, evolution and release: a full life.

No Moment Past This One

I tell you, it seems always to be out there.
Is it like a blanket? No, it is nothing
like a blanket. Is it like darkness?
No, neither is it like darkness. But it
doesn't act like something within me.
How do I know this? Because it seems
to be waiting. And it seems to have both
hunger and humor. And it seems both
patient and eager, ponderous and weightless.
And it is large. And it grows larger. How

can it not be like darkness when it devours
the light? How can it not be like a blanket
when it seems so all-enveloping? How
can it seem like a place to tumble into
and still be so tireless, so agile? Yet if I
could answer such riddles, then perhaps,
perhaps, but when it comes it wraps me
in silken ropes, and it draws the life from me
and yet I continue to breathe, even though
I feel there is no moment past this one
and this one, and the days continue to pass.
You see, it must come from someplace outside,
some cold place or from deep in the earth,
because if the beast dwelt within me, then
how could I live, how could it be withstood?

For Liz Rosenberg

A Postmortem Guide

For my eulogist, in advance

Do not praise me for my exceptional serenity.
Can't you see I've turned away
from the large excitements,
and have accepted all the troubles?

Go down to the old cemetery; you'll see
there's nothing definitive to be said.
The dead once were all kinds —
boundary breakers and scalawags,
martyrs of the flesh, and so many
dumb bunnies of duty, unbearably nice.

I've been a little of each.

And, please, resist the temptation
of speaking about virtue.
The seldom-tempted are too fond
of that word, the small-
spirited, the unburdened.
Know that I've admired in others
only the fraught straining
to be good.

Adam's my man and Eve's not to blame.
He bit in; it made no sense to stop.

• • •

Still, for accuracy's sake you might say
I often stopped,
that I rarely went as far as I dreamed.

And since you know my hardships,
understand they're mere bump and setback
against history's horror.
Remind those seated, perhaps weeping,
how obscene it is
for some of us to complain.

Tell them I had second chances.
I knew joy.
I was burned by books early
and kept sidling up to the flame.

Tell them that at the end I had no need
for God, who'd become just a story
I once loved, one of many
with concealments and late-night rescues,
high sentence and pomp. The truth is

I learned to live without hope
as well as I could, almost happily,
in the despoiled and radiant now.

You who are one of them, say that I loved
my companions most of all.
In all sincerity, say that they provided
a better way to be alone.

Burying the Cat

Her name was Isadora and, like all cats,
she was a machine made of rubber bands
and muscle, exemplar of crouch

and pounce, genius of leisure. 17 years old.
A neighbor dog had broken her back,
and the owner called when he saw my car
pull into the driveway. He'd put her
in a plastic sack. It was ridiculous
how heavy she was, how inflexible.
For years I've known that to confess
is to say what one doesn't feel. I hereby
confess I was not angry with that dog,
a shepherd, who had seen something foreign
on his property. I'd like to say I was feeling
a sadness so numb that I was a machine myself,
with bad cogs and faulty wiring. But
I'm telling this three years after the fact.
Nothing is quite what it was
after we've formed a clear picture of it.
Behind our house there's a field, a half-acre
of grass good for the sailing of a frisbee.
I buried her there. My thought was to do it
before the children came home from school,
my wife from work. I got the shovel
from the shed. The ground was not without
resistance. I put several stones on top,
pyramid style, a crude mausoleum. What
we're mostly faced with are these privacies,
inconsequential to all but us. But I wasn't
thinking that then. I kicked some dirt
off the shovel, returned it to the shed.
I remember feeling that strange satisfaction
I'd often felt after yardwork, some evidence
of what I'd done visible for a change.
I remember that after their shock, their grief,
I expected to be praised.

Oklahoma City

The accused chose to plead innocent
because he was guilty. We allowed such a thing;
it was one of our greatnesses, nutty, protective.
On the car radio a survivor's ordeal, her leg
amputated without anesthesia while trapped

under a steel girder. Simply, no big words —
that's how people tell their horror stories.
I was elsewhere, on my way to a party.
On arrival, everyone was sure to be carrying
a piece of the awful world with him.

Not one of us wouldn't be smiling.
There'd be drinks, irony, hidden animosities.
Something large would be missing.
But most of us would understand
something large always would be missing.

Oklahoma City was America reduced
to McVeigh's half-thought-out thoughts.
Did he know anything about suffering?
It's the innocent among us who are guilty
of wondering if we're moral agents or madmen

or merely, as one scientist said,
a fortuitous collocation of atoms.
Some mysteries can be solved by ampersands.
Ands not *ors*; that was my latest answer.
At the party two women were talking

about how strange it is that they still like men.
They were young and unavailable, and their lovely faces
evoked a world not wholly incongruent
with the world I know. I had no illusions, not even hopes,
that their beauty had anything to do with goodness.

Poe in Margate

To come back and learn his alcoholism
was an illness — Poe had to laugh at that.
He knew the vanity of excuses better than anyone,
and how good self-destruction feels when one
is in the act of it. Still, he thought, you must be sober
to write your autobiography, set things straight.

He'd give up all notions of a kingdom by the sea,
try to see things as they were and are.
But soon came the old, constant rebellion
of the senses and mind, soon he remembered
that truth was an enormous house shrouded in mist
with many secret vaults, and that perfect sobriety

is the state in which you make the version of yourself
you like best, just another way to lie. He'd have
just one drink before dinner to ease in the night,
and from his window watch monstrous Lucy the Elephant
closing up, tourists no longer walking in her body
and looking out of her eyes. The world was stranger

than he had imagined it, certainly no less strange.
The newspaper that arrived daily at his doorstep
was storied with men who murdered because voices
told them to, girls who killed their newborns
then returned to the prom. In his autobiography
he'd insist on the ultimate sanity of the artist,

regardless of what he did with his life. He'd tell
of his long hours of calculation and care,
how when Usher's house fell into that tarn
it was a victory of precision over the loose ends
of a troubled mind, how his insane narrators needed
everything that was rational in him all of the time.

Chekhov in Port Republic

No one but I took special notice of his presence,
and he hadn't come to heal, unless to render
the residual sorrow behind all our pretensions
is to heal. He was as attentive to torpor
as he was to vitality, and he knew
how pretty words and big promises could swindle,
not unlike how the church fools the poor.

Some of us had seen his black satchel, had heard
he'd helped the Jenkins woman late one night
when, bruised and bleeding, she knocked on his door.
In the old country many men beat their wives,
blaming it on vodka or weather. He didn't believe
geography made much difference; we were all the same.
And he, well he was in the business of making things

imperishable, and none of us, finally, could be saved.
He'd said the best stories require a cold eye,
his fellow humans frozen in the folly of being themselves.
But of course he tended to her wounds.
Bandages were what a doctor used. The writer
in him wanted the world made visible, exposed.

He'd rented the Olsen house set back off Chestnut.
Sometimes a lady with a dog would be seen in the driveway,
though it was presumed he lived alone.
I had no trouble believing that the dead travel
between two worlds, like wind, like minds.

And I was honored such a great writer had chosen
my town. I'd read his work, saw the photos of him
before he got sick. He was Chekhov all right.
And there was enough misery here,
enough Potemkin-like facades, to give him new life.

The Dig

Beyond the dark souks of the old city, beyond the Dome of the Rock
gray and humped and haunted, beyond the eyes of the men at the café
where they drink their thimblefuls of hot tea, beyond the valley
with its scar of naked pipe, the perfect geometrical arcs of irrigation,
and someone incising a dark furrow in a field, some plowman's black
gutter opening through the green, she is waist deep in this open grave,
staring at the delicate puzzle of my feet. Beyond her, in the shadow
of Tel Hesi, daubing and dampening the earth, another woman finds
the faint brickwork of floor spidering the dust, on the hearth's
wedge-shaped arc of shadow a scattering of charred millet.
Nothing else for miles. Nothing but this bluff of ruin,
one decapitated tower, one "window" staved into the brick,
the bougainvillea crawling across a wall dragging its little bloody rags.
She is standing here thinking she cannot bear the way this foot —
my foot — wants to step out of the earth. I don't care. I am using her
to leave the grave, and the trowel hits stone and I lie staring
while she makes the earth recede, reaches in and pulls me out,
my jaw wired shut by roots, my skull so full of dirt that suddenly
the intricate sutures come loose and, in her hands, the whole head opens.
In the shallow setting where I lay is the small triangular sail
of a scapula, the ribs like the grill of a car. She bones me like a fish.
She lays the little pieces, the puzzling odds and ends, into the dishes
of shellac and formalin. Wearily, I lean my reassembled head,
sutures rich with glue, against the wall of the filled beaker.
A fine sweat of bubbles on my chin. All night, through the window
of my jar, I watch her mend with glue and wire the shallow
saucer of my pelvis. We are nothing. Earth staring at earth.

The Burial

After I've goosed up the fire in the stove with *Starter Logg*
so that it burns like fire on amphetamines; after it's imprisoned,
screaming and thrashing, behind the stove door; after I've
listened to the dead composers and watched the brown-plus-gray
deer compose into Cubism the trees whose name I don't know
(pine, I think); after I've holed up in my loneliness staring
at the young buck whose two new antlers are like a snail's
stalked eyes and I've let this conceit lead me to the eyes-on-stems
of the faces of Picasso and from there to my dead father; after I've
chased the deer away (they were boring, streamlined machines
for tearing up green things, deer are the cows-of-the-forest);
then I bend down over the sea of keys to write this poem
about my father in his grave.

It isn't easy. It's dark in my room, the door is closed,
all around is creaking and sighing, as though I were in the hold
of a big ship, as though I were in the dark sleep
of a huge freighter toiling across the landscape of the waves
taking me to my father with whom I have struggled
like Jacob with the angel and who heaves off, one final time,
the muddy counterpane of the earth and lies panting
beside his grave like a large dog who has run a long way.

This is as far as he goes. I stand at the very end
of myself holding a shovel. The blade is long and cool;
it is an instrument for organizing the world; the blade is
drenched in shine, the air is alive along it, as air is alive
on the windshield of a car. Beside me my father droops
as though he were under anesthesia. He is so thin,
and he doesn't have a coat. My left hand grows
cool and sedate under the influence of his flesh.
It hesitates and then . . .

My father drops in like baggage into a hold.
In his hands, written on my stationery, a note
I thought of xeroxing: *Dad, I will be with you,*

through the cold, dark, closed places you hated.
I close the hinged lid, and above him I heap a
firmament of dirt. The body alone, in the dark,
in the cold, without a coat. I would not wish that on my
greatest enemy. Which, in a sense, my father was.

inside gertrude stein

Right now as I am talking to you and as you are being talked to, without letup, it is becoming clear that gertrude stein has hijacked me and that this feeling that you are having now as you read this, that this is what it feels like to be inside gertrude stein. This is what it feels like to be a huge typewriter in a dress. Yes, I feel we have gotten inside gertrude stein, and of course it is dark inside the enormous gertrude, it is like being locked up in a refrigerator lit only by a smiling rind of cheese. Being inside gertrude is like being inside a monument made of a cloud which is always moving across the sky which is also always moving. Gertrude is a huge galleon of cloud anchored to the ground by one small tether, yes, I see it down there, do you see that tiny snail glued to the tackboard of the landscape? That is alice. So, I am inside gertrude; we belong to each other, she and I, and it is so wonderful because I have always been a thin woman inside of whom a big woman is screaming to get out, and she's out now and if a river could type this is how it would sound, pure and complicated and enormous. Now we are lilting across the countryside, and we are talking, and if the wind could type it would sound like this, ongoing and repetitious, abstracting and stylizing everything, like our famous haircut painted by Picasso. Because when you are inside our haircut you understand that all the flotsam and jetsam of hairdo have been cleared way (like the forests from the New World) so that the skull can show through grinning and feasting on the alarm it has created. I am now, alarmingly, inside gertrude's head and I am thinking that I may only be a thought she has had when she imagined that she and alice were dead and gone and someone had to carry on the work of being gertrude stein, and so I am receiving, from beyond the grave, radioactive isotopes of her genius saying, take up my work, become gertrude stein.

Because someone must be gertrude stein, someone must save us from the literalists and realists, and narratives of the beginning and end, someone must be a river that can type. And why not I? Gertrude is insisting on the fact that while I am a subgenius, weighing one hundred five pounds, and living in a small town with an enormous furry male husband who is always in his Cadillac Eldorado driving off to sell something to people who do not deserve the bad luck of this merchandise in their lives — that these facts would not be a problem for gertrude stein. Gertrude and I feel that, for instance, in *Patriarchal Poetry* when (like an avalanche that can type) she is burying the patriarchy, still there persists a sense of condescending affection. So, while I'm a thin, heterosexual subgenius, nevertheless gertrude has chosen me as her tool, just as she chose the patriarchy as a tool for ending the patriarchy. And because I have become her tool, now, in a sense, gertrude is inside me. It's tough. Having gertrude inside me is like having swallowed an ocean liner that can type, and, while I feel like a very small coat closet with a bear in it, gertrude and I feel that I must tell you that gertrude does not care. She is using me to get her message across, to say, I am lost, I am beset by literalists and narratives of the beginning and middle and end, help me. And so, yes, I say, yes, I am here, gertrude, because we feel, gertrude and I, that there is real urgency in our voice (like a sob that can type) and that things are very bad for her because she is lost, beset by the literalists and realists, her own enormousness crushing her, and we must find her and take her into ourselves, even though I am the least likely of saviors and have been chosen perhaps as a last resort, yes, definitely, gertrude is saying to me, you are the least likely of saviors, you are my last choice and my last resort.

The White Dress

What does it feel like to be this shroud
on a hanger, this storm cloud hanging
in the closet? We itch to feel it, it itches
to be felt, it feels like an itch —

encrusted with beading, it's an eczema
of sequins, rough, gullied, riven,
puckered with stitchery, a frosted window
against which we long to put our tongues,

.   .   .

a vase for holding the long-stemmed
bouquet of a woman's body.
Or it's armor and it fits like a glove.
The buttons run like rivets down the front.

When we're in it we're machinery,
a cutter nosing the ocean of a town.
Right now it's lonely locked up
in the closet; while we're busy

fussing at our vanity, it hangs there
in the drooping waterfall of itself,
a road with no one on it, bathed
in moonlight, rehearsing its lines.

All the People in Hopper's Paintings

All the people in Hopper's paintings walk by me
here in the twilight the way our neighbors
would stroll by of an evening in my hometown
smiling and waving as I leaned against
the front-porch railing and hated them all
and the place I had grown up in. I smoked
my Pall Mall with a beautifully controlled rage
in the manner of James Dean and imagined
life beyond the plains in the towns of Hopper
where people were touched by the light of the real.

The people in Hopper's paintings were lonely
as I was and lived in brown rooms whose
long, sad windows looked out on the roofs
of brown buildings in the towns that made
them lonely. Or they lived in coffee shops
and cafés at three a.m. under decadent flowers
of cigarette smoke as I thought I would have
if there had been such late-night conspiracy
in the town that held me but offered nothing.
And now they gather around with their bland,

mysterious faces in half-shadow, many still
bearing the hard plane of light that found them
from the left side of the room, as in Vermeer,
others wearing the dark splotches of early
evening across their foreheads and chins that said
they were, like me, tragic, dark, undiscovered:
the manicurist from the barber shop buried
beneath a pyramid of light and a clock frozen

at eleven, the woman sitting on the bed
too exhausted with the hopelessness of brick walls

and barber poles and Rhinegold ads to dress
herself in street clothes. The wordless, stale
affair with the filling station attendant
was the anteroom to heartbreak. The gloom
of his stupid uniform and black tie beneath
the three white bulbs blinking MOBILGAS into
the woods that loomed bleak as tombstones
on the edge of town; the drab backroom
with its Prestone cans and sighing Vargas girls
and grease rags; his panting, pathetic *loneliness*.

But along the white island of the station,
the luminous squares from its windows
lying quietly like carpets on the pavement
had been my hope, my sense then of the real world
beyond the familiar one, like the blazing café
of the nighthawks casting the town into shadow,
or the beach house of the sea watchers
who sat suspended on a verandah of light,
stunned by the flat, hard sea of the real.
Everywhere was that phosphorescence, that pale

wash of promise lifting roofs and chimneys
out of dullness, out of the ordinary that I
could smell in my workclothes coming home
from a machine shop lined with men who stood
at lathes and looked out of windows and wore
the same late-afternoon layers of sunlight
that Hopper's people carried to hotel rooms
and cafeterias. Why was their monotony
blessed, their melancholy apocalyptic, while
my days hung like red rags from my pockets

as I stood, welding torch in hand, and searched
the horizon with the eyes and straight mouth

of Hopper's women? If they had come walking
toward me, those angels of boredom, if they
had arrived clothed in their robes of light,
would I have recognized them? If all those women
staring out of windows had risen from their desks
and unmade beds, and the men from their offices
and sun-draped brownstones, would I have known?
Would I have felt their light hands touching

my face the way infants do when people
seem no more real than dreams or picture books?
The girl in the blue gown leaning from her door
at high noon, the gray-haired gentleman
in the hotel by the railroad, holding his cigarette
so delicately, they have found me, and we
walk slowly through the small Kansas town
that held me and offered nothing, where the light
fell through the windows of brown rooms, and people
looked out, strangely, as if they had been painted there.

The Machinist, Teaching His Daughter to Play the Piano

The brown wrist and hand with its raw knuckles and blue nails
        packed with dirt and oil, pause in mid-air,
the fingers arched delicately,

and she mimics him, hand held just so, the wrist loose,
        then swooping down to the wrong chord.
She lifts her hand and tries again.

Drill collars rumble, hammering the nubbin-posts.
        The helper lifts one, turning it slowly,
then lugs it into the lathe's chuck.

. . .

The bit shears the dull iron into new metal, falling
*   into the steady chant of lathe work,*
and the machinist lights a cigarette, holding

in his upturned palms the polonaise he learned at ten,
*   then later the easiest waltzes,*
études, impossible counterpoint

like the voice of his daughter he overhears one night
        standing in the backyard. She is speaking
to herself but not herself, as in prayer,

the listener is some version of herself,
        and the names are pronounced carefully,
self-consciously: Chopin, Mozart,

Scarlatti, . . . these gestures of voice and hands
        suspended over the keyboard
that move like the lathe in its turning

toward music, the wind dragging the hoist chain, the ring
        of iron on iron in the holding rack.
His daughter speaks to him one night,

but not to him, rather someone created between them,
        a listener, there and not there,
a master of lathes, a student of music.

Old Men Playing Basketball

The heavy bodies lunge, the broken language
of fake and drive, glamorous jump shot
slowed to a stutter. Their gestures, in love
again with the pure geometry of curves,

.   .   .

rise toward the ball, falter, and fall away.
On the boards their hands and fingertips
tremble in tense little prayers of reach
and balance. Then, the grind of bone

and socket, the caught breath, the sigh,
the grunt of the body laboring to give
birth to itself. In their toiling and grand
sweeps, I wonder, do they still make love

to their wives, kissing the undersides
of their wrists, dancing the old soft-shoe
of desire? And on the long walk home
from the VFW, do they still sing

to the drunken moon? Stands full, clock
moving, the one in army fatigues
and houseshoes says to himself, *pick and roll,*
and the phrase sounds musical as ever,

radio crooning songs of love after the game,
the girl leaning back in the Chevy's front seat
as her raven hair flames in the shuddering
light of the outdoor movie, and now he drives,

gliding toward the net. A glass wand
of autumn light breaks over the backboard.
Boys rise up in old men, wings begin to sprout
at their backs. The ball turns in the darkening air.

The Great Gizzardo

Gizzard dentata: minuscule rocks which chickens
and ducks, with a squawk, swallow. Understand

they don't have teeth like ours. They keep a pouch
of hard objects (including bullets and coins)

to break down what they eat, make it
useful. Think what goes on

in the dark of their bodies: a mystery
mills around the farmer's boots

as he looks to the sky. And the mystery
is there too, in the ethersphere,

inside the always-watchful baldy birds
that fly in circles, waiting for a weak calf,

or me, or you, to drop. Finally, come slaughter
time, the magic teeth of poultry gleam (wet

with blood), then get tossed to a garbage can. Let us
take this moment to hear the grindgrindgrind —

the Great Gizzardo doing his job. Even now
the gears of the clock are nibbling us small.

Lord of the Jungle, Larva-Nude

The loincloth, the lionkills — all that came later:
Tarzan's teen years were an endless PE class.
He envied the hairiness of his Great Ape peers;

worse, their balls big as coconuts. He felt
sick sneaking up behind a girl chimp
for a schtup, and fled. He panicked a clique

of crocodiles by rolling a rock from the top
of a hill. He sulked a lot. Life improved
when he found a knife in his father's house.

Herkimer, Mohawk, et al., in Autumn

Postcards show the warm oranges and reds —
the leaves of upstate New York Octobers —
but don't do justice to the boondock towns:
Mohawk, Herkimer, Hornell, Norwich. . . . Hey,

is that where Norwich aspirin are made?
Aspirin dissolve luxuriously as dunes
to erase (almost) the lines on a brow. . . .
White particles whir through the blood, sleep comes. . . .

But what's it like for workers in that factory?
Does bonedust fizz the air, and boredom toll
in their skulls? Of course they dream of travel
and Kama Sutra stunts, that's what a person does. . . .

Every year the trees grow tired of green —
there's not much time, the crones-to-be go wild —
every year the leaves make our most fervid
yearnings visible, flagrant, harder to take. . . .

. . .

Soon, come the winter's whiteout, a woman
mindful of the colors will get a pang
each time she sees a stained glass window,
or Christmas lights, or her boy's comic books.

Australia

Never been there, but I have seen
on maps the continent, brain-shaped —
a feverish brain of a place broken
free from Gondwanaland long ago

and so become a Darwin farm
for oddball beauties. Eggs cascade
from the platypus's furry ass!
A just-born kangaroo, the size
of a grub, must wriggletrek up
its mother's belly to her pouch.
My point is, these fragile-yet-sturdy
freaks evolved in the world's boondocks
but nowhere else. It's wonderful,

in that way, to be off by oneself.
In solitude, new possibilities breed.

But other times, alone, I tend to want
the TV on, or to leaf through magazines.
Really, in Australia a vast desert
dominates the green. I looked at a map.

What We Wait For

Saddlebags bulging with envelopes,
parcels, a pony express rider's steed
galloped up a cloud of dust. From faraway

it appeared a voracious see-through
serpent was on the verge of engulfing
its source. . . . A hostile, hovering spirit

seemed to mouth horse and man. . . . Now,
what's your dustcloud? What's the nimbus
the knowledge of which precedes you?

What's your name? Well, it's beside the point.
We wait and wait for the orphaned rider out
of breath; and what he brings to us, unknown.

Faces Underwater

Deep end of the pool, a boy
does the jellyfish float, watching

all the lapswimmers. Their arms carve
holes in the H_2O; their legs kick up bubbles

like a boat propellor. But their faces,
even better. . . . There's the retired Captain

who's had two heart attacks, goddammit,
and vowed to pummel his bulk up and down

one lane till he's a welterweight. He'll be
a specimen. Already his breath, expelled,

• • •

transforms his face, making it a silver mask
of exertion, hot-looking, demonic. . . .

His is the face one learns to hide, ambition-
or fearface pure as an acetylene torch. . . .

And then the boy is forced to surface:
loud world, where laughter can be heard.

Bang!

When I was splitting the wood with
agreeable violence and accuracy, settled
into full-arc swings of the sledge, bang
on the long blue wedge, bang upon the red,

splitting the big trunk rounds of maple
into lengths little thicker than kindling,
my neighbor offered, over the fence,
that I was "doing that with a vengeance."

Maybe, partly, and why not? If I can
still swing it so, at 52, as, probably,
I won't be able to in 10 years, even 5,
Bang! few pauses, Bang! all afternoon.

Well, vengeance on what? — How about
death and aging and marriage and flesh
and grief and writing and money and death:
bottomless pits, pitiless bottoms.

But *mostly* just to accept, to a steady beat,
the gifts of timing and strength and
precision: Bang!-swing it-Bang!-swing it-
Bang! Goddamned hard. All afternoon.

Wake

In the gunny dusk of a dream
the old man looks too small
for his best blue suit — as he
lies in state, or as he boards
the train to bear him away.
"Wait," says the dreamer,
still adream or awake,
like a voice reaching idly
after his father, who glances
with fitful resentment
but doesn't wait.

It could be the passenger car
of a country train, its steps
painted black, its skinny sweep
of hand-rail brass, the rest
dull green. Or else he lies
where all his get were got,
where the old man and mother
lay, struggled, and slept for
fifty-five years. Is he propped
there or getting aboard? — both
are in the dream —

And other choices. But propped
up there or boarding, the dream
smells gumbo: of depot, of potato
warehouse or subway, of turnip,
dry-rot, sweat. And the malign
and abused old man does not
look up from the bed where he
lies, or down from the steps
but turns away to mount the
train, his fixed face all
sallow-creased and gray.

• • •

The bed has grown or the old man,
though fatter in old age, grows
smaller in death's reprise.
Its fake brass frame of hollow
tubes may be the handrail on
the train, but its springs
are deeply silent, formal,
all turned to catafalque.
Stilled too the old man's
ripping voice, even its late
susurring lisp is gone.

But broken and softened by dying,
sunken down into this repose of
death's fat baby, the face still
speaks its power, balefully, of
his father. And whether glaring
away from the dreamer, or refusing
all solace from the bed, propped
or climbing, he lies where he lies
or mounts where he mounts, alone,
in the gunny dusk of the dream.

Spring

How little it can take
To finish winter —
Jonquil blossoms break
Outside, she brings
A dozen in, and from
The pitcher yellow sings.

Barukh ata adonay

What is this new breathlessness,
when you lie down, a symptom of?
Like, if not as bad as, what you felt,
on your back, in Laramie, fish-gasping,
seven thousand feet above sea-level.
But now, back home, the earth flat,
the ocean near, you still pant
when you first lie down. It's better
if you sit a while first, easing
to prone, and say, instead of timing
the descent, Hebrew blessings
on bread and wine. Anyway, such
prayers, if not the words themselves
(or God), somewhat relieve the scare:
the relaxed time they take to say,
but silently, without effort, these
Barukhim on your breath, old man.

Nothing Doing

Stub of December, the year in a fast fade.
Christmas trees dragged stump-first to the curb,
clumps of wrinkled tinsel the only glitter.

All else — grass, sky — dead yellow,
all else wan and resigned, the black, burnt out
wick of the year too weak to raise a flame.

Everything looking a little late and left behind:
power line slumped and swinging in a stiff breeze,
wheelchair abandoned beneath the off-ramp,

two-by-four moldering in a ditch, its single
bent nail like a rusty finger bone.
Grackle perched on a mailbox, staring

at nothing. He's right to take a hard look.
I always miss it, too: the turn, the wheeze
of one year becoming the whispered

intimation of a new one, the world's furniture
suddenly in a new room without moving.
It's now, with strict attention, one might

detect the mechanism: the webbed intricacy
of the grackle's brain, the planets stirring up
their circles of dust. Perhaps it's now we're nearest

• • •

to something that could save us — something
beyond our knowledge and our will to believe it.
The day is stark, hushed, ground down

to particulars, as if encrypted.
Time to watch for a sign, a shift. When
nothing happens, I'll have my proof.

The Fidgeting

Easy to make prayers to the darkness, to break bread
with the inconceivable. Harder to love

the moon — dusty dead-white relic
in the star museum, bald and obvious

as a drunken uncle. Hard to find worth
in the crooked pine that creaks

outside the kitchen window, every twig
a wagging finger as it lectures

on the miracle of the physical world.
Any day is the same day — the hours

writhe like worms in a bucket.
One can be an astonished infant

for only so long before the fidgeting,
before a flock of blackbirds bursting

from poplars, or a sodden collection
of fallen leaves blown against a fence,

. . .

is wearisome. Even the stiff, bloated opossum
by the roadside is only a brief diversion

before one longs to follow the opossum-soul,
to know where it goes and how it fares

in the province it scuttles off to,
the who-knows-where, anywhere but here.

Gouge, Adze, Rasp, Hammer

So this is what it's like when love
leaves, and one is disappointed
that the body and mind continue to exist,

exacting payment from each other,
engaging in stale rituals of desire,
and it would seem the best use of one's time

is not to stand for hours outside
her darkened house, drenched and chilled,
blinking into the slanting rain.

So this is what it's like to have to
practice amiability and learn
to say the orchard looks grand this evening

as the sun slips behind scumbled clouds
and the pears, mellowed to a golden-green,
glow like flames among the boughs.

It is now one claims there is comfort
in the constancy of nature, in the wind's way
of snatching dogwood blossoms from their branches,

. . .

scattering them in the dirt, in the slug's
sure, slow arrival to nowhere.
It is now one makes a show of praise

for the lilac that strains so hard to win
attention to its sweet inscrutability,
when one admires instead the lowly

gouge, adze, rasp, hammer —
fire-forged, blunt-syllabled things,
unthought-of until a need exists:

a groove chiseled to a fixed width,
a roof sloped just so. It is now
one knows what it is to envy

the rivet, wrench, vise — whatever
works unburdened by memory and sight,
while high above the damp fields

flocks of swallows roil and dip,
and streams churn, thick with leaping salmon,
and the bee advances on the rose.

The Actual Moon, The Actual Stars

In that hour of boundless night when dark
tugs at me with its bustle and fuss

and the grass outside my window, gone
a deep blue, chirrs and clicks with crickets

and my thoughts flop and twitch
like fish in a galvanized bucket

. . .

and sweat soaks the sheets, collecting
in drops down my spine and behind my knees,

I like to leave my bones and flesh
lying in the bed while I roam the neighborhood,

only my being, the big idea of myself,
out for a stroll. I go undetected

by the sensor light in the side yard
and any dog or possum that crosses my path.

I go past the parked cars and clusters
of mailboxes, houses hunkered down

in the dark, an occasional light
whitening a single window. I go

without breath or breathlessness, I go
with forgiveness in my invisible heart

for the frail forms imposed upon
disorder: the painted stones a neighbor

has bordered his yard with, the black
plastic garbage bins

wheeled to the ends of driveways. I let
my mind forget its wrestling match

with the flesh, its urge to account for the burden
of the body by making of it an allegory.

I let whatever story I'm in
unfold its plot without interruption,

• • •

though chances are it is not a tale
about my welfare, and I cannot say

I comprehend what the least part of it
means, the bits of gravel scattered

on the blacktop glinting like stars, the battered
bottle cap glowing like a small fallen moon —

above, the actual moon, the actual stars
shining like nothing but themselves.

The St. Louis Zoo

The isle is full of noises
Sounds, and sweet airs . . . sometimes voices.
— *The Tempest*

High, yellow, coiled and weighting the branch like an odd piece of fruit, a
                                                    snake slept
by the gate, in the serpent house. I walked around the paths hearing

hushed air, piecemeal remarks, and the hoarse voice of the keeper spreading
                                                    cabbage
and pellets in the elephant compound — "Hungry, are you? There's a girl.
                                                    How's Pearl?"

A clucking music, then silence again crept past me
on the waters of the duck pond. Birds with saffron wings in the flight cage

and flamingos the color of mangoes, even their webbed feet red-orange,
                                                    made so
"by the algae they ingest," as angels are made of air — some bickered,

some were tongue-tied, some danced on one leg in the honeyed light.
I thought of autumn as leaves scattered down. Nearby, closed away

in his crude beginnings in a simulated rain forest, the gorilla pulled out
                                                    handfuls
of grass, no Miranda to teach him to speak, though he was full of noises

. . .

and rank air after swallowing. Smooth rind and bearded husks lay about
him.
His eyes were ingots when he looked at me.

In late summer air thick with rose and lily, I felt the old malevolence;
the snake tonguing the air, as if to tell me of its dreaming: — birds of
paradise

gemming a pond; the unspooling; soft comings on, soft, soft
gestures, twisted and surreptitious; the shock; the taste; the kingdom.

In something more than words, *You are the snake, snake coils in you,*
it said. Do you think anyone knows its own hunger as well as the snake?

Why am I not just someone alive? When did Spirit tear me
to see how void of blessing I was? The snake hesitated, tasting dusk's black
honey,

to feel if it was still good. And through its swoon
it knew it. Leaf, lichen, the least refinements, and the perfection.

Komodo

The flight of a white cockatoo from tamarind to tamarind
still in his mind's eye, one morning, Baron von Biberegg lay down

like a streak of flowers in the dust. Lush mist, animal calls & birds sinking,
the mind
breeding without moving — O sleep, O golden hive. Then a giant lizard

appeared. When? Within an hour. In modern times.
As out of a dream's monstrous whirlpooling,

the monitor with flaming, olfactory tongue probing the air,
consumed the Baron — hands, ivory teeth and bones, skin and fabric — ,

• • •

whose sap mounted in terror or disbelief, groaned, spilled, then sank into
$\qquad\qquad\qquad\qquad\qquad\qquad$ the ground,
the sun deranged in the fronds.

————————

To be utterly missing, given over like drying rain,
so that at some point his wife had to give up grieving,

his companions searching the bamboo groves, *tanah panas*, the unplumbed,
hot, estranging forests, then placing the white cross

to mark their last glimpse of him, and to tell themselves
he *had* been, his having-died filling them like abundance . . .

— wasn't he already a part of the dragon, visible in the yellow eyelids,
septic teeth, clawed feet solid as the bottoms of brass table legs?

Sentinel, snare, spirit, devourer, relative of the ascending bird.

————————

And the Promethean feasting; the shaking of the fragile frame
through sunrise and day, the throbbings through nighttime.

No one there to see the mouth tremble or to hear his thoughts.
Soul winces — as though divinity *could* be drained from him.

Yet Prometheus, yet the risings and settings of the stars we know
to follow, yet all the instructive frenzy lives

leaf by leaf, step by step, in the brandishing moment
and in the way the mountains and the savannas are waiting —

as the mind waits, the startled little bees that leap below sense and unseen.
Also fragments of liver, spoiling in the air, propose defiance.

————————

And the ones who study the monitor lizard, while deer lie
napping in the azyma bushes? — the ones for whom Orpheus' music

carries little sting or sweetness as they watch, in bird cry and tambourine
of sunlight, the lizards tongue the white fecal pellets of their rivals, and hold

the tongue and lashing tail in their hands for measurement? For them
neither heart nor devil nor god figure; no perfidy in the reptile's ambush; no
metaphor;

only viscera, anatomy, the echoing straits between Indonesian islands,
isolation and escape.
Lizards prowl, eat, and mate, trued by the tips of their tails.

They lie in the grass or in their holes, with head outside the mouth
of the burrow and eyes wide open, staring into the black surrounding forest.

If this is it, if they completely inhabit themselves, there are no morals
or excuses. None for the disemboweled, disembodied: goats, pigs, horses,
the blazing cockatoo, the pink, lightless, inner tissues of the Baron.

Compatibility

Never after was life so filled with meeting,
with reuniting and drawing apart as then, when bed-hot, filled with surges,
the man and woman began to know each other.
It was like the makeshift walking of geese toward water, — a settling into
themselves and,
with a fiercer and fiercer grip, a testing of the untried other. How safe they'd
been before
they touched and he asked her *one* thing which she meant to resist but was
unable to.
How beautiful to keep one's fabled eyes closed: — Was another's body not
like some bright
obstruction? But they, as if they knew nothing, opened entirely, bending to
two wills,

striking down vanities, feeling what lay deep inside — the darker

compatibilities —

until love seemed causal, not just related.

Their sinuous tongues used the word, over and over, without speaking.

Scorn

She thought of no wilder delicacy than the starling eggs she fed him for

breakfast,

and if he sat and ate like a farmhand and she hated him sometimes,

she knew it didn't matter: that whatever in the din of argument

was harshly spoken, something else done soothed and patted away.

When they were young the towering fierceness

of their differences had frightened her even as she longed for an almost

physical release.

Out of their mouths such curses; their hands huge, pointing, stabbing the

air.

How had they *not* been wounded? And wounded they'd convalesced in the

same rooms

and bed. When at last they knew everything without confiding — fears,

stinks,

boiling hearts — they gave up themselves a little so that they might both love

and scorn

each other, and they ate from each other's hands.

Requin

If in memory a pulse of music swims

with the great white shark, what notes for autumn

withering, and what signature for ground

. . .

swell — slow, cerebral, or horns' crescendo?
To wear the white skin of the coming snow
and hear the palsied cries of finches, how

else to know absence? To hear *ritardando*
in ebbing tide, and ghosting red tones
in the dawn. As silence requires music,

so death requires requiem, a lyric
resting in the eternal: the shark
in French is *requin*, an allusion to

the silent white deadliness; consonants
for being, for swimming with a body
in the jaw, for the startling return

to darker tones after so much clear blue.
To become more clear-eared before nature.
Even Cézanne's last paintings of nature,

*Pistachio Tree at Chateau Noir, Mont
Sainte-Victoire,* in purifying whites make
the unheard world: silences before vows

sung under the breath, and after tone rows
of fresh wind in pistachio boughs.
Sunlight is ivory, locks of the artist's

fine hair, and you nearly can hear his voice
as he paints the mauve and white and moist
purple of mountains. Listen. Listen hard.

Blue Annunciation

Tawny hay bales on
            the tan mown slope

Distant cypresses on hunched
            ridges like black candle flames

The sea as dark as purple grapes

Ozone scent of ordinary
            fierce geraniums and hot
thick pungency of meek petunias

Obsessive announcements of a hidden dove

There's a word for the
            color of the clear sky
but none for the falling-away-
            upward depth of it
that feels too spanning and
            speeding from us
for us ever to have called
            into it in time

And for what purpose down the
            hundred thousand generations —
from carved magic
            bone to machine gun
from daubed red ochre to
            acres of robbed riverbeds —

. . .

did our perceiving, when it
        comes into us
fully, into our hollows,
        become in itself such pleasure?

Ghazal

Archeologist of feeling, would-be soothsayer of candor,
I work in the sun while I listen for thunder.

I see a coyote trot across a meadow slope, alert and calm,
Like a mind for both the wild rose and the soaring condor.

Time that crawls over everything turns what is
To what was, and creates in us our sense of wonder.

We make love and unmake it, and we ask,
Why did she spurn him? Why did he wound her?

In summer, worshipped sunlight comes clear through green stems
To praise the exploring ant whose only work is to wander.

In autumn, willow leaves migrate to the ground, the geese
Fall southward, a letter homes to me marked "Return to Sender."

Some poplar that lives about as long as I will stand for me,
Will wait in line as I write in lines, until we both go under.

If there comes a day when I can advance no further,
It's because on that day I have no father, no mother, no founder.

I slant through wildernesses and cities of our common cause
That say, Reg, you must be persistent, undiscouraged, and tender.

I Not I

You cupped the gushing water in my palms
You walked the miles with my determination
You listened for the first sound of night with my ears
You did the job with my sore hands and stumbling feet

You spoke the words with my lips and tongue
You drank with my gulping thirst
You rushed up the wooded slope with my legs and lungs
At the top you felt the cold wind against my skin

You counted your breaths with my attention
Greedily you tasted through my nose
And mouth the scents of flowers and infants
You pushed my breath with my gut into your shout

You canvassed for signatures with my persuasiveness
You hitchhiked to the demonstration with my thumb
With my politics you studied the crowds and speakers
Then you walked the real avenues with my questions in mind

You brought forth the images in my thoughts
You beat the blood through my body with my heart
You used my eyes to see the woman's beautiful nakedness
You entered the woman's beautiful *cunnan* with my *dictare*

You lifted the heavy red grief and carried it in my arms
You felt my pain as the stab wounds healed
You groped through my mental fog for the needed word
You lost the thread of my thinking

You took what you wanted with my appetite
You tore and chewed meat and anger with my teeth
You swallowed hard with my throat
You used my bowels to push shit out

• • •

To you, things happened in my dreams
You fevered the heat of my desires and fears
With my musicianship you played the piano
You wrote the pages with my right hand

With the excuse of my fatigue you stopped creating
You found it hard to avoid the ambiguity
of statement that permits an easier interpretation
You found it hard to straiten the passage

in order to permit only the difficult interpretation
that is singular, elusive and at least somewhat enduring
You were not a god or a spirit but you arrived through me
You were not I but you arrived only through me

Down There, If You Look

Standing lightly, precariously, almost
Floating, don't
Shift your weight even slightly,
Over jagged raw holes in the floor
Of time.
        Down there, if you look . . .

Down there, blue clouds float against
A white sky; great walls and high buildings
Are only deep muddy ditches at the bottom of which
Squatting women are taking their babies
Back into their wombs and standing men
Tilt their heads up as they eat
Long floating ribbons of words.

Envoi

Go, little book, tell of

Rainstorm thunderclap; icy gale; breaking waves;
The rushing movement out there —
Markets; threshers; presses; lobbies and hallways —
Against which we feel the stillness inside us;

Snow quiet; clear night sky; northern summer dawn;
The stillness out there —
Empty barns and shipyards; construction sites and kitchens at three
a.m. —
Against which we feel the rushing inside us.

Mock Orange

It is not the moon, I tell you.
It is these flowers
lighting the yard.

I hate them.
I hate them as I hate sex,
the man's mouth
sealing my mouth, the man's
paralyzing body —

and the cry that always escapes,
the low, humiliating
premise of union —

In my mind tonight
I hear the question and pursuing answer
fused in one sound
that mounts and mounts and then
is split into the old selves,
the tired antagonisms. Do you see?
We were made fools of.
And the scent of mock orange
drifts through the window.

How can I rest?
How can I be content
when there is still
that odor in the world?

Celestial Music

I have a friend who still believes in heaven.
Not a stupid person, yet with all she knows, she literally talks to god,
she thinks someone listens in heaven.
On earth, she's unusually competent.
Brave, too, able to face unpleasantness.

We found a caterpillar dying in the dirt, greedy ants crawling over it.
I'm always moved by weakness, by disaster, always eager to oppose vitality.
But timid, also, quick to shut my eyes.
Whereas my friend was able to watch, to let events play out
according to nature. For my sake, she intervened,
brushing a few ants off the torn thing, and set it down across the road.

My friend says I shut my eyes to god, that nothing else explains
my aversion to reality. She says I'm like the child who buries her head in the
    pillow
so as not to see, the child who tells herself
that light causes sadness —
My friend is like the mother. Patient, urging me
to wake up an adult like herself, a courageous person —

In my dreams, my friend reproaches me. We're walking
on the same road, except it's winter now;
she's telling me that when you love the world you hear celestial music:
look up, she says. When I look up, nothing.
Only clouds, snow, a white business in the trees
like brides leaping to a great height —
Then I'm afraid for her; I see her
caught in a net deliberately cast over the earth —

In reality, we sit by the side of the road, watching the sun set;
from time to time, the silence pierced by a birdcall.
It's this moment we're both trying to explain, the fact
that we're at ease with death, with solitude.
My friend draws a circle in the dirt; inside, the caterpillar doesn't move.
She's always trying to make something whole, something beautiful, an image

capable of life apart from her.
We're very quiet. It's peaceful sitting here, not speaking, the composition
fixed, the road turning suddenly dark, the air
going cool, here and there the rocks shining and glittering —
it's this stillness that we both love.
The love of form is a love of endings.

The Wild Iris

At the end of my suffering
there was a door.

Hear me out: that which you call death
I remember.

Overhead, noises, branches of the pine shifting.
Then nothing. The weak sun
flickered over the dry surface.

It is terrible to survive
as consciousness
buried in the dark earth.

Then it was over: that which you fear, being
a soul and unable
to speak, ending abruptly, the stiff earth
bending a little. And what I took to be
birds darting in low shrubs.

You who do not remember
passage from the other world
I tell you I could speak again: whatever
returns from oblivion returns
to find a voice:

. . .

from the center of my life came
a great fountain, deep blue
shadows on azure seawater.

Ithaca

The beloved doesn't
need to live. The beloved
lives in the head. The loom
is for the suitors, strung up
like a harp with white shroud-thread.

He was two people.
He was the body and voice, the easy
magnetism of a living man, and then
the unfolding dream or image
shaped by the woman working the loom,
sitting there in a hall filled
with literal-minded men.

As you pity
the deceived sea that tried
to take him away forever
and took only the first,
the actual husband, you must
pity these men: they don't know
what they're looking at;
they don't know that when one loves this way
the shroud becomes a wedding dress.

Nest

A bird was making its nest.
In the dream, I watched it closely:

in my life, I was trying to be
a witness not a theorist.

The place you begin doesn't determine
the place you end: the bird

took what it found in the yard,
its base materials, nervously
scanning the bare yard in early spring;
in debris by the south wall pushing
a few twigs with its beak.

Image
of loneliness: the small creature
coming up with nothing. Then
dry twigs. Carrying, one by one,
the twigs to the hideout.
Which is all it was then.

It took what there was:
the available material. Spirit
wasn't enough.

And then it wove like the first Penelope
but toward a different end.
How did it weave? It weaved,
carefully but hopelessly, the few twigs
with any suppleness, any flexibility,
choosing these over the brittle, the recalcitrant.

Early spring, late desolation.
The bird circled the bare yard making
efforts to survive
on what remained to it.

It had its task:
to imagine the future. Steadily flying around,
patiently bearing small twigs to the solitude

of the exposed tree in the steady coldness
of the outside world.

I had nothing to build with.
It was winter: I couldn't imagine
anything but the past. I couldn't even
imagine the past, if it came to that.

And I didn't know how I came here.
Everyone else much farther along.
I was back at the beginning
at a time we can't remember beginnings.

The bird
collected twigs in the apple tree, relating
each addition to existing mass.
But when was there suddenly *mass?*

It took what it found after the others
were finished.
The same materials — why should it matter
to be finished last? The same materials, the same
limited good. Brown twigs,
broken and fallen. And in one,
a length of yellow wool.

Then it was spring and I was inexplicably happy.
I knew where I was: on Broadway with my bag of groceries.
Spring fruit in the stores: first
cherries at Formaggio. Forsythia
beginning.

First I was at peace.
Then I was contented, satisfied.
And then flashes of joy.
And the season changed — for all of us,
of course.

. . .

And as I peered out my mind grew sharper.
And I remember accurately
the sequence of my responses,
my eyes fixing on each thing
from the shelter of the hidden self:

first, *I love it.*
Then, *I can use it.*

The Education

I used to, when the children were little, travel
everywhere by public transport with them,
into "the city" and back
or out to the end of the line to "the country" and back
without getting off. We'd go
for the sake of the journey, to see
and be seen in the world, to be part of the large picture,
the boys in sailor suits, the girl and I
in matching pinafores. We'd go
to touch some hearts, to strike some chords,
all of us in the same so-to-speak lifeboat
S.S. Humanity, I'd explain to the children,
and somebody near would say, "Amen to that,"
and somebody else, "Never again a Hitler."
We'd go, too, for the jig and the jog of the ride,
and for the pull of the brakes
and for the squealing,
and for the naming aloud of subway stations
the children learned by heart and enjoyed chanting
forward and backward, as if those places loved them,
as if their little lungs could power the vehicle,
as if they weren't the bird the snake was swallowing,
as if we were going somewhere.

I Was Looking

through a crevice at the hunger children
when my hands
dropped from my wrists.

I was looking at the hunger children feeding
on a squirrel's bones
when both my hands, my gentle hands, my dear
caressing doves
fell down.

I was wearing gloves.
I was looking at the hunger children
chewing on their mothers' thighs.
Two-button kidskins and the children's mouths
engaged in mother eating
when my hands
dropped to my lap
and twitched like just dead lobsters. I was

looking. I was thinking
oranges and apples when
my hands in rich white kidskin gloves
the elegant postbellum length
detached like milktree pods and I

was blowing kisses on my severed hands,
my creamy sausages, my once
warm touch knots
when the children bit

the wormy center of their appetites
dying like children in a photograph
which, rubbing lotion
on my stump ends,
I was looking at.

What They Are

1. they are small they are fat there are many of them
   you can touch them they can touch you

   they are death

   all your life you have been speaking about death
   as if you had nothing better
   to do with your mouth
   then speak about that
   thinking death was what would happen once to anyone but

   they are small they are ripe they are mad about you
   you can squeeze them they are in-
   destruct-
   ably soft
   tomatoes
   beginning
   to be rancid
   like your own
   soft
   underarms

   they have faces
   they have eloquent faces
   when you step on their faces they cry out
   they cry out EEYOW YOU ARE HURTING US BADLY
   as if you had hurt them

   there are many of them
   in the gut in the hair at the root of the tongue
   in the rain in the moon in the dust of the parking lot crying

   WE ARE YOUR BABIES AND WHY
   WERE WE DUMPED FROM THE FREIGHT TRAIN

   . . .

WE ARE YOUR FINGERS REMEMBER
YOU PROMISED YOU PROMISED

2. today is your birthday
   (good morning good morning)
   the guests are arriving
   you never invited

   arriving like hemorrhoids
   you never invited
   but daily created
   (the rubbing the rubbing)

   like bullets arriving
   the better to eat you
   (delicious delicious)
   your sin and your virtue

   the better to know you
   they drink from your blisters
   (l'chaim l'chaim)
   they blow out your wishes

   their gift is the mortgage
   you snatch from their fingers
   (oh shylocks sweet shylocks)
   they lend you your life

The Visitation

I sipped from your glass to take my own
medicine. I wasn't sick, only
hurting locally. You were sick all over

. . .

but recovering: "a little better
every week" the friends who saw you weekly
tried to persuade you. Still and all

it was a grim scenario — and for me, no picnic,
having released you, having to reach back
to recathect you as a between-deaths person,

your intelligence reconstituted between deaths
but your eyes, tenants in death's sockets.
"It's snowing out," I said. You said, "Is it?"

That's when I went to the edge of your couch, to face
what you'd been facing, blurred windows
expressing nothing, or nothing much. Ghosts, I ventured.

They'd gathered at your windows meaning well,
not meaning to cancel your view of the skyline, but.
All erasures are the same erasure, the same wipe.

That morning, as my plane entered the cloudbank
I thought back fifty years to Miss Gray's classroom.
On the board, a poem that had to be copied fast

before she'd say, "Time's up!" and turn it to chalkdust.
It wasn't like me to reach for your glass that way.
I'd said, "Do you mind?" and you'd said, "Go ahead."

Later, we spoke of *germs;* we shrugged them off.
Later still, I thought about *milk, wine, hemlock;*
also, *a kind of kiss* — and that felt closer
to the metaphysic of the act, for which I am still reaching.

The Knife Accuses the Wound

The knife accuses the wound: *See how I bleed,*
to which the wound replies: *We bleed as one.*
That's how it was between us, between her and me

when one of us was the cloth and one the needle;
one the teeth, the other one the tongue.
Knife to wound: *See how I bleed.*

Bough to cradle: *You tore me from the tree.*
Cradle to broken bough: *You let me down.*
That's how it was between us, between her and me

when the wind shifted from the south to the northeast
and stone by stone her house fell into ruin.
The knife accuses the wound: *See how I bleed,*

and the needle the cloth, the tongue the teeth,
and cradle and bough one another in lieu of the wind.
That's how it was between us, between her and me,

each of us talking in the other's sleep
mouth against mouth until the end of being,
the knife still accusing the wound: *See how I bleed.*
That's how it was between us, between her and me.

Grammatical Mood

1.
There is, to her mind, only one.
       Or only
      one that's built to scale. Had we known

sooner. Had the only man to whom the CAT scan
       yielded
      so much detailed information not

been out of town that week. Had those few sticky
       platelets moved
      with just a shade more expedition through

the infant artery. . . . The parallel life
       will not
      relent. But look, we may say to her, Look

at them tied to their breathing machines, they do not
       cry
      (because of the tubes you'll say, you're right, to you

the silence is dreadful). To you the vicious
       calculus
      abides no counter-argument: the oxygen

that supplements their unripe lungs destroys
       the retina,
      leaving the twice-struck child in darkness. What

. . .

must they think of us, bringing them into a world
        like this?

2.

        For want of an ion the synapse was lost.

For want of a synapse the circuit was lost.
        For want
        of a circuit, the kingdom, the child, the social

smile. And this is just one of the infinite means by which
        the world
        may turn aside. When my young daughter, whose

right hand and foot do not obey her, made us take
        off
        the training wheels, and rode and fell and pedaled

and fell through a week and a half of summer twilights
        and finally
        on her own traversed the block of breathing maples

and the shadowed street, I knew
        what it was like
        to fly. Sentiment softens the bone in its socket. Half

the gorgeous light show we attribute to the setting sun
        is atmospheric
        trash. Joy is something else again, ask Megan

on her two bright wheels.

3.

        To live
        in the body (as if there were another

. . .

place). To graze among the azaleas (which are
          poison
          to humans, beloved by deer; not everything

the eye enjoys will sit benignly on the
          tongue). It must
          have been a head shot left her ear at that

frightening angle and the jaw all wrong,
          so swollen
          it's a wonder she can chew. Is that

where they aim, the good ones, when they're
          sober? At
          the head? At a doe? The DNR biologist is

saintly on the phone, though God knows he's not chiefly
          paid
          to salve the conscience (I have

bad dreams) of a gardening species stricken by
          its own
          encroachment. Fecundity starveth

the deer in the forest. It fouls the earth it
          feeds upon.
          Fecundity plants the suburban azalea, which

dies to keep the damaged deer in pain. I mean
          alive.

4.
          For want of rain the corn was lost.

For want of a bank loan we plowed up the windbreak
          and burnt it
          (you must learn to think on a different scale, they told

• • •

us that). For want of a windbreak and rainfall
        and corn
            the topsoil rose on the wind and left. God's own

strict grammar (imperative mood). I meant
        to return
        to joy again. Just

give me a minute. Just look at the sky.

Cord

OTG 1912–1994

Dearest, we filled up the woodroom
        this week,
          Karen and Steven and I and Peter's

truck. You would have been amused
        to see us in our
        woodsman's mode. It's your wood still.

You know those homely cruxes where the odd piece,
        split
        near the fork for instance, has to be turned

till it's made to fit and another
        lame one
        found for the gap? Sap

just yesterday, smoke in the end, this
        clubfoot
        marking the meantime. I came

. . .

to one of them, one of the numberless
        justnesses
      a life of stacking wood affords (had you even

broken rhythm?) and for just that instant
        had you back.
      I know. I know. It wasn't the last, despite

the strangled heaving of your chest, despite
        the rattled
      exhalation and the leavened, livid, meat-

borne smell, it wasn't the last till afterward, I've
        made that
      my excuse. But Mother was sleeping not five

feet away, she'd scarcely slept in weeks, I could
        have
      waked her. I (sweet darling, the morphine

under your tongue) am much (your quiet
        hands)
      to blame. And when we had dismantled this last-

but-one of the provident stores you'd
        left —
      a winter's worth of warmth in each —

and hauled it in, we split and stacked the new
        oak Peter
      felled last spring. We took a day off in

between, we wrapped ourselves in virtue, we
        can be
      good children yet. The gingkos

  • • •

have come back from their near
          poisoning, have
       I told you that? Our tenant's

remorseful, he's sworn off new insecticides. My
          hour with you (one
       breath, one more) was theft.

Submersible

Why art thou cast down, O my soul? — Psalm 42

Down from twilight into dark at noon,
through darker, down until the black
could not be more devoid of star
or sunlight, O my soul, near freezing
in sub-photic stillness past
the fragile strands of glowing jelly
radiant with tentacles to sting,
and bioluminescent lures of anglers,
down where water beading on the cold hatch
overhead has sheathed in dewdrops
the titanium, past dragonfish
with nightlights set into their heads
and flanks, past unlit cruisers,
blackcod, owl fish, eelpout, skate,
where spider crabs, arms long as mine,
on creamy prongs drift floodlit
over the pillow lava, here,
our craft has taken us where no one
could have come till now but corpses.

I Am

And he hath put a new song in my mouth, even praise
unto our God . . . — Psalm 40

The fog I call the world is not a cloud of atoms
only, but a cloud of feelings, and ideas. I mind
my little bumps. I grieve. I think about non-being.
All I do is what my flesh can do, yet everything
my flesh can do feels strange. I am the swelling
of a salt sea onto an armature of chalk, the calm
of a tidal pool where brain cells live, the wind,
the lightning storm where thought flares into thought.
I taste damp sparks inside my tongue. If sayings
gather under the name of Faith, or Art, I let them
when they let me let them, and my mind clears.

Sackcloth

I made sackcloth also my garment; and I became a proverb
to them. They that sit in the gate speak against me; and
I was the song of drunkards. — Psalm 69

I made sackcloth my garment once, by cutting
arm and neck holes into a burlap bag.
A croker sack they called it. Sackdragger
they called a man who dragged a croker sack
between the cotton rows to pick. He dragged
a gunnysack behind him in the ditch
collecting empties. Him they chose
the Likeliest to Sack Seed in the feed store,
or to suck seed. He was your daddy. He sacked
groceries part-time, and they jeered:
you sorry sack of shit. Sackcloth,
which Job sewed upon his skin, was goat hair.
God clothed the heavens with blackness,
and he said, I make sackcloth their covering.

Isaiah understood. God had him speak a word
in season to the weary. Speak, Isaiah, now, to me.
Before the stars like green figs in a windstorm
drop, the sun is black as sackcloth, and the moon
becomes as blood. My soul is weary. Speak,
Isaiah. Sing. I was a scholar as a boy:
I cut the neck and arm holes into the burlap,
pulled it on, and cinched it with a hank of rope:
what I have done from then till now is itch.

God's World, 1927

He hath founded it upon the seas, and established it upon the
floods. — Psalm 24

After the flood spilled over the sandbags on the levee,
each bag placed where one was needed burst. The bags
weighed half what men did. Men kept filling them,

and carrying them uphill, to be set where now they burst
that instant. All night, in a freezing downpour, poor
white men with pistols, shivering and cursing, had made

black men, sharecroppers and convicts, tote the bags.
The few men shot dead running washed away. Others
were prevailed upon to sing. They sang in praise

of outlaws and of God. To the west a big uprooted
cottonwood raked over the underwater tops of willows.
Dawn. East, thirty feet below flood crest stood shacks

. . .

and mansions. Black men (hundreds, freezing, muscles
aching them) and white men (holding them at gunpoint),
all, could feel foretremblings in the ground

about to be pushed out from under them. They saw,
at seven thirty, Thursday, April twenty-first, the wall
of earth come open. Then, the cataclysm (with nobody-knows-

how-many men) broke over the fields where tall pecan trees
snapped, shacks tumbled, shattered, mules screamed.
And the psalm says, Be ye lift up, O, ye everlasting doors.

Rotgut

The sun shall not smite thee by day, nor the moon
by night. — Psalm 121

Under a hillside scattered with temples broken
by the dogday sun, my friend and I drank
local wine at nightfall and ate grapeleaves
in goat-yogurt glaze. The living grape vines
bore fruit overhead. Beyond our balcony,
beyond the Turkish rooftops, an old moon
touched Venus at one tip. This vintage,
he said, would melt pig iron. But I wondered,
were we drunk enough, and he said no. I took him,
staggering and laughing, in my arms, and soon,
with snow at nightfall easing off,
another old moon slid into the hill
behind my dead friend's house. He loved
that smear of light cast back on it from earth.

Scrolls

So will I compass thine altar, O Lord:
that I may publish with the voice of
thanksgiving. — Psalm 26

Thine altar is to me this bathtub
where my four-year-old twin
girls tip back their heads.
They close their eyes.
I read their faces from above,
in trust and fear, in holiness,
heads tipped until the waterline
has touched their hairlines, cautious.
Look: their hair flows underwater
like the scrolls unfurled in heaven.

The Desire Manuscripts

1. The Craving

(*The Odyssey*, Book Twelve)

I needed a warning from the goddess
and a group of men to lash me to the mast
hand and foot, so that I could listen
to swelling, sun-scorched, fatal voices
of two Sirens weaving a haunted sound
over the boiling surf, calling me downward
while I twisted with desire in the ropes
and pleaded to be untied, unbound, unleashed.
How willingly I would have given myself up
to that ardor, that drowning blue charm,
while hopeless clouds scudded overhead
and the deaf oarsmen rowed ruthlessly home.
I was saved, I know, but even now, years later,
I crave those voices dreaming in my sleep.

2. What the Goddess Can Do

(*The Odyssey*, Book Ten)

Maybe it was the way she held her head
or her voice, which was too high, or her braids,
which reminded me of a girl I used to know,

. . .

but I sat on a tall chair like a god
drinking a bowl of honey mulled with wine
and getting drowsy, counting my good fortune,

so that she could transform me into a pig
squealing for acorns, grunting and bristling
in a sty, snouting the ground with other swine.

Later, our leader convinced her to reverse
the spell, setting our animal bodies free . . .

I have been many things in this life —
a husband, a warrior, a seer — but I cannot forget
what the goddess can do to me, if she desires.

———————

3. The Sentence

(*Inferno*, Canto Five)

When you read Canto Five aloud last night
in your naked, sing-song, fractured Italian,
my sweet compulsion, my carnal appetite,

I suspected we shall never be forgiven
for devouring each other body and soul,
and someday Minos, a connoisseur of sin,

will snarl himself twice around his tail
to sentence us to life in perpetual motion,
funneling us downward to the second circle

where we will never sleep or rest again
in turbulent air, like other ill-begotten
lovers who embraced passion beyond reason,

. . .

and yet I cannot turn from you, my wanton;
our heaven will always be our hell, a swoon.

———————

4. In the Mourning Fields

(*The Aeneid*, Book Six)

The world below is starless, stark and deep,
and while you lay beside me, my golden bough,
plunged into the shadowy marsh of sleep,

I read about the infernal realm, and how
a soldier walked forth in the House of Dis
while still alive, breaking an eternal law

by braving death's kingdom, a vast abyss,
the ground sunken in fog — eerie, treacherous —
guarded by a mad beast, three-throated Cerberus.

Tonight I read about us — foundering, hopeless —
in the Mourning Fields and the myrtle grove,
wandering on separate paths, lost in darkness.

It is written that we were consumed by love,
here on earth, a pitiless world above.

———————

5. After All the Orphic Enchantments

(*The Metamorphosis*, Books Ten and Eleven)

After all the Orphic enchantments, after all
was said and done, after a second death stunned
and claimed his wife for the fluttering clouds
and phantom forms, the misting lower depths,

• • •

after he pleaded with Charon for a second chance
but was dismissed and chased above ground
where he shunned women for a good three years
and notched a life for himself with young men,

a vegetarian priest who recited the passions
of lovers who paid for their transgressions —
the Cerastes, the Propoetides, Pygmalion,
Myrrha and Cinyras, Venus and Adonis —

after everything was closed, completed,
and the costs were tallied, after he sang
for the hyacinths and virgin laurels
and charmed the drooling souls of beasts,

after he enraged the Thracian women who
circled like birds of prey and ripped him
into pieces, as the gods had prophesied,
after his body watered the ground with blood

and currents carried his severed head chanting
downstream with such a spellbinding grief
that trees shed leafy crowns and stones leapt
up and swollen rivers wept in their beds,

I wonder if Orpheus ever decided it was
worth it after all, relinquishing his body
so he could return to the nether world
which he knew by heart and where, I hope,

he moves with Eurydice on the other side,
a shade still singing amid the other shades,
sometimes walking behind her, sometimes ahead,
and swiveling round to gaze at her forever.

———————

6. The Regret

(The Lost Orphics)

If we had never married, if you had never strolled
barefoot through high grass with a poisonous snake
that sent you weeping alone into the underworld

to join the other shades, the fresh new recruits
arriving at all hours at the waystation of eternity,
Persephone's insubstantial realm, the House of Death,

and if I, who could entrance the Stygian fog
and convince the god of our ravishing need for
each other, here and now, in the world above,

had never turned back for my limping wife ·
on a shadowy path out of utter silence,
the void of Avernus, the margins of earth,

then I might not be floating here alone
on a mournful hillside, devoid of shade,
praising young boys beloved by the fates

to the approaching trees, the bright lotus,
lover of pools, and the bittersweet hazel,
the river-haunted willow and the mountain ash,

awaiting my own death, the crazed Furies
who will send my head and my lyre downstream
still singing about us, what might have been.

America

Then one of the students with blue hair and a tongue stud
Says America is for him a maximum security prison whose walls

Are made of Radio Shacks and Burger Kings, and MTV episodes
Where you can't tell the show from the commercials,

And as I contemplate how full of shit I think he is,
He says that even when he's driving to the mall in his Isuzu

Trooper with a gang of his friends, letting rap music pour over them
Like a boiling jacuzzi full of ballpeen hammers, even then he feels

Buried alive, captured and suffocated in the folds
Of the thick satin quilt of America

And I wonder if this is a legitimate category of pain,
Or whether he is just spin-doctoring a better grade,

And then I remember that when I stabbed my father in the dream last night,
It was not blood but money

That gushed out of him, bright green hundred-dollar bills
Spilling from his wounds, and, this is the funny part,

He gasped, "Thank God — those Ben Franklins were
Clogging up my heart —

And so I perish happily,
Freed from that which kept me from my liberty" —

. . .

Which is when I knew it was a dream, since my dad
Would never speak in rhymed couplets

And I look at the student with his acne and cell phone and phony ghetto clothes
And I think, "I am asleep in America too,

And I don't know how to wake myself either"
And I remember what Marx said near the end of his life:

"I was listening to the cries of the past,
when I should have been listening to the cries of the future"

But how could he have imagined 100 channels of 24-hour cable
Or what kind of nightmare it might be

When each day you watch rivers of bright merchandise run past you
And you are floating in your pleasure boat upon this river

Even while others are drowning underneath you
And you see their faces twisting in the surface of the waters

And yet it seems to be your own hand
Which turns the volume higher?

Carnal Knowledge

The night your girlfriend
first disappeared beneath the sheets
to take you in her red, wet mouth,
with an amethystine sweetness
and a surprising expertise,

. . .

then came up for a kiss as her reward,
you had to worry whether you could taste
the faint flavor of your own
penis on her soft peach lips —

and what that possibly could mean
was an idea so charged
it scorched the fragile circuits
of your eighteen-year-old imagination,

though by now you were beginning to suspect
that everyone lived a secret life
of acts they never advertised,
and you were right.

Maybe that was the evening you began to learn
how to swallow
what you couldn't understand
in the name of love

what it felt like to be entered
by something strange
for pleasure's sake.

And afterwards, did you look
into the distance of the dark,
and smoke a cigarette
and feel a little foreign to yourself?

as someone does who has been changed
by a single unexpected drop of life?

Lucky

If you are lucky in this life
you will get to help your enemy

the way I got to help my mother
when she was weakened past the point of saying no.

Into the big enamel tub,
half-filled with water
which I had made just right,
I lowered the childish skeleton she had become.

Her eyelids fluttered as I soaped and rinsed
her belly and her chest,
the sorry ruin of her flanks
and the frayed gray cloud
between her legs.

And some nights, sitting by her bed,
book open in my lap,
while I listened to the air
move thickly in and out of her dark lungs,
my mind filled up with praise
as lush as music,

amazed at the symmetry and luck
that would offer me the chance to pay
my heavy debt of punishment and love
with love and punishment.

And once, after her bath,
I held her dripping in the uncomfortable
air between the wheelchair and the tub,
until she begged me like a child to stop,

an act of cruelty
which we both understood
as the ancient, irresistible rejoicing
of power over weakness.

If you are lucky in this life,
you will get to raise the spoon

of pristine, frosty ice cream
to the trusting creature mouth
of your old enemy

because the tastebuds at least are not broken
because there is a bond between you
and sweet is sweet in any language.

Lawrence

On two occasions in the past twelve months
I have failed, when someone at a party
spoke of him with a dismissive scorn,
to stand up for D. H. Lawrence,

a man who burned like an acetylene torch
from one end to the other of his life.
These individuals, whose relationship to literature
is approximately that of a tree shredder

to stands of old growth forest,
these people leaned back in their chairs,
bellies full of dry white wine and the ova of some foreign fish,
and casually dropped his name

the way that pygmies with their little poison spears
strut around the carcass of a fallen elephant.
"Oh elephant," they say,
"You are not so big and brave today!"

It's a bad thing when people speak of their superiors
with a contempt they haven't earned
and it's a sorry thing when certain other people

don't defend the great dead ones
who have opened up the world before them.

And though, in the catalogue of my betrayals,
this is a fairly minor entry,

I resolve, if the occasion should recur,
to uncheck my tongue and say "I love the spectacle
of maggots condescending to a corpse,"
or, "You should be so lucky in your brainy bloodless life

as to deserve to lift
just one of D. H. Lawrence's urine samples
to your arid psychobiopornographic
theory-tainted lips."

Or maybe I'll just take the shortcut
between the spirit and the flesh,
and punch someone in the face,
because human beings haven't come that far

in their effort to subdue the body,
and we still walk around like zombies
in our dying, burning world
able to do little more

than fight, and fuck, and crow,
something Lawrence wrote about
in such a manner
as to make it seem magnificent.

Jet

Sometimes I wish that I was still out
on the back porch, drinking jet fuel
with the boys, getting louder and louder
as the empty cans drop out of our paws
like booster rockets falling back to earth

. . .

and we soar up into the summer stars.
Summer. The big sky river rushes overhead,
bearing asteroids and mist, blind fish
and old space suits with skeletons inside.
On earth, men celebrate their hairiness

and it is good, a way of letting life
out of the box, uncapping the bottle
to let the effervescence gush
through the narrow, usually constricted neck.

And now the crickets plug in their appliances
in unison, and then the fireflies flash
dots and dashes in the grass, like punctuation
for the labyrinthine, untrue tales of sex
someone is telling in the dark, though

no one really hears. We gaze into the night
as if remembering the bright unbroken planet
we have come from, to which we will never
be permitted to return.
We are amazed how hurt we are.
We would give anything for what we have.

Prayer

Lord of the branches, who made the goat and the waterbug
Lord of the whale and whatever is — wind and ash and planet and
   honeybee . . .

I sit before you, distracted, growing older, without any clothes on
my hair pinned up with barrettes —

Every day I want to speak with you. And every day something more important
calls my attention — the drug store, the beauty products, the luggage

I need to buy for the trip — Even now I can hardly sit here
among the falling piles of paper and clothing, the garbage trucks already

screeching and banging. The day will be hot,
the sky deep secular blue. The mystics say you are as close as my own breath
   — why

do I flee from you? My days and nights pour through me like complaints
and become a story I forgot to tell. Help me. Even as I write these words I am

planning to rise from the chair as soon as I finish this sentence.

A Certain Light

He had taken the right pills the night before.
We had counted them out

. . .

from the egg carton where they were numbered so there'd be no mistake.
He had taken the morphine and prednisone and amitriptyline

and Florinef and vancomycin and Halcion too quickly
and had thrown up in the bowl Joe brought to the bed — a thin string

of blue spit — then waited a few minutes, to calm himself,
before he took them all again. And had slept through the night

and the morning and was still sleeping at noon — or not sleeping.
He was breathing maybe twice a minute, and we couldn't wake him,

we couldn't wake him until we shook him hard calling, John wake up now
John wake up — Who is the president?

And he couldn't answer.
His doctor told us we'd have to keep him up for hours.

He was all bones and skin, no tissue to absorb the medicine.
He couldn't walk unless two people held him.

And we made him talk about the movies: What was the best moment in
On the Waterfront? What was the music in *Gone with the Wind?*

And for seven hours he answered, if only to please us, mumbling
I like the morphine, sinking, rising, sleeping, rousing,

then only in pain again — but wakened.
So wakened that late that night in one of those still blue moments

that were a kind of paradise, he finally opened his eyes wide,
and the room filled with a certain light we thought we'd never see again.

Look at you two, he said. And we did.
And Joe said, Look at you.   And John said, How do I look?

And Joe said, Handsome.

Reading Ovid

The thing about those Greeks and Romans is that
    at least mythologically,

they could get mad. If the man broke your heart, if he
    fucked your sister speechless

then real true hell broke loose:
    "You know that stew you just ate for dinner, honey?

It was your son."
    That's Ovid for you.

A guy who knows how to tell a story about people who
    really don't believe in the Golden Rule.

I sometimes fantasize saying to the man I married "You know
    that hamburger you just

gobbled down with relish and mustard? It was
    your truck"

if only to watch understanding take his face
    like the bird-god took the girl.

But rage makes for more rage: nothing to do then but run.
    And because rage is a story that has

no ending, we'd both have to transform into birds or fish
    constellations forever fixed

in the starry heavens: forever separated,
    forever attached.

Remember the story of Athens and Sparta?
    That boy held the fox under his cloak

. . .

and didn't flinch. A cab driver told me the part
    I couldn't remember this morning.

In Sparta, he said, it was permissible to steal
    but not to get caught.

The fox bit and scratched; the kid didn't talk
    and he was a hero.

Do unto others as you would have them do unto you,
    Jesus said, and they hammered

the nails through his wrists. The kingdom of heaven
    is within you, he said,

and the spiked wheel turned over
    the living centuries, minute by minute, soul by soul,

turns still. That's the good news and the bad news, isn't it?
    No one need ever be lonely again.

Practicing

I want to write a love poem for the girls I kissed in seventh grade,
a song for what we did on the floor in the basement

of somebody's parents' house, a hymn for what we didn't say but thought:
That feels good or *I like that*, when we learned how to open each other's mouths

how to move our tongues to make somebody moan. We called it practicing,
    and
one was the boy, and we paired off — maybe six or eight girls — and turned
    out

the lights and kissed and kissed until we were stoned on kisses, and lifted our
nightgowns or let the straps drop, and, Now you be the boy:

. . .

concrete floor, sleeping bag or couch, playroom, game room, train room,
    laundry.
Linda's basement was like a boat with booths and portholes

instead of windows. Gloria's father had a bar downstairs with stools that spun,
plush carpeting. We kissed each other's throats.

We sucked each other's breasts, and we left marks, and never spoke of it
    upstairs
outdoors, in daylight, not once. We did it, and it was

practicing, and slept, sprawled so our legs still locked or crossed, a hand still
    lost
in someone's hair . . . and we grew up and hardly mentioned who

the first kiss really was — a girl like us, still sticky with the moisturizer we'd
shared in the bathroom. I want to write a song

for that thick silence in the dark, and the first pure thrill of unreluctant desire,
just before we made ourselves stop.

What the Living Do

Johnny, the kitchen sink has been clogged for days, some utensil probably fell
    down there.
And the Drano won't work but smells dangerous, and the crusty dishes have
    piled up

waiting for the plumber I still haven't called. This is the everyday we spoke
    of.
It's winter again: the sky's a deep headstrong blue, and the sunlight pours
    through

. . .

the open living room windows because the heat's on too high in here, and
  I can't turn it off.
For weeks now, driving, or dropping a bag of groceries in the street, the
  bag breaking,

I've been thinking: This is what the living do. And yesterday, hurrying
  along those
wobbly bricks in the Cambridge sidewalk, spilling my coffee down my wrist
  and sleeve,

I thought it again, and again later, when buying a hairbrush: This is it.
Parking. Slamming the car door shut in the cold. What you called *that
  yearning.*

What you finally gave up. We want the spring to come and the winter to
  pass. We want
whoever to call or not call, a letter, a kiss — we want more and more and
  then more of it.

But there are moments, walking, when I catch a glimpse of myself in the
  window glass,
say, the window of the corner video store, and I'm gripped by a cherishing so
  deep

for my own blowing hair, chapped face, and unbuttoned coat that I'm
  speechless:
I am living, I remember you.

Do Not Leave Baby Unattended

Manufacturer's Warning

There is a Maker
who refuses to be sued, a presence
among us which does not wish

to be believed in, or leaned on, or seen.
He drops a small
seed in the earth — fruitful, dutiful, blind —

and it is me. But the earth
around it is also me. He names me
This One's Mother, and there

will never be
any other who could share
a liability. *If anything.*

If something . . .
The unspeakable lodges itself
like a boiling coin of blood on the tongue.

Even if I die, this one is mine. My faith
is a dove
asleep in the slaughterhouse eaves.

My attention
is a net
sewn of smoke and weight. Even

. . .

if I died, my eyes would have to be
always open underground, or blinking
in the sky. Who-

ever you are, up all night
embroidering warnings and disclaimers
on our things, sleep

easy, please. I cannot
sue you, I cannot
even die: Some nights

are darker than trees. The sky
in their hair breathes. There is
no one in this house

when the lights are out
but the great blameless Maker,
and the child,

and the Mother attending these.

Joy

I stayed in bed for days and watched
a spider in the light spin
an airy web above my head, something

cool and loose, without
the use of force, or weight.

That time, I nearly died

. . .

of joy. I was a child. Still alive.
Relatives stood above me smiling. Summer
was my sickness. Translucent

nurses brought me everything
I needed, while I

swam in and out of sun, which
unraveled its white knitting
on the surface of the pool, and flew

above the orchards, which stretched
in bloom
from my mind to the end of time — just
above the branches, but at great speed

and thought I saw a small girl running
like a madwoman beneath the trees.

I didn't even need to eat! I *drank* the beautiful meals
my mother made for me

from coolness and silver spoons. My father
sat at the edge of the bed
and prayed for the angels' protection. Like

talcum and masculine sweat, the smell
of wet feathers as I slept. I got better

and better, listening . . .

But what was that sound? The clock? The toilet

flushing? Rain on the playground? The ocean
choking on its own waves?

No.

• • •

It was a dog
lapping at a bloody tray.

Childhood came and went in a day

and I woke on Sunday in the arms of a stranger.
Oh, I realized then,

this must be joy again. Despite

the headache, the salty thirst, the shame — that

spinning above the bed, more
light than thread, was

exactly, *exactly*, the same.

Small Boys Petting Caterpillar

Somewhere, a God
is handling our hearts.
Wonder can kill, accidentally, what it loves.

It's summer. The ditches
are full of fish-scales and glitter. Also
the sepulcher, the tomb, the pit. Someone
has scraped them out of the air

with the dull edge of a knife. Someone

has told them to be gentle, and now
their little hands are light as prayers. If
they breathe, their hands will float away.
The music of dust in water.

. . .

One of them is trembling. One

is bouncing with his legs crossed.
Perhaps he needs to pee.

Above us, on the highest limb, a dangerous piece of fruit dangles.
A teenage girl is stepping

all over the sunshine in her silver shoes. Perhaps

that piece of fruit will simply
drift into her hands.
It did, for me. Swiftly,
but with wings.

And the caterpillar

is a word, a soft bit of star. Oblivious, our hearts. Could
that word be *faith*, or *trust*, or is it

some other word which means
to let go in ignorance, or *to hold one's breath and hope*?
And would that word be *love*?

It doesn't matter because
we're helpless in the hands of what does.

The Satyr's Heart

Now I rest my head on the satyr's caved chest,
The hollow where the heart would have been, if sandstone
Had a heart, if a headless goat man could have a heart.
His neck rises to a dull point, points upward
To something long gone, elusive, and at his feet
The small flowers swarm, earnest and sweet, a clamor
Of white, a clamor of blue, and black, the sweating soil
They breed in . . . If I sit without moving, how quickly
Things change, birds turning tricks in the trees,
Colorless birds and those with color, the wind fingering
The twigs, and the furred creatures doing whatever
Furred creatures do. So, and so. There is the smell of fruit
And the smell of wet coins. There is the sound of a bird
Crying. And the sound of water that does not move . . .
If I pick the dead iris? If I wave it above me
Like a flag, a blazoned flag? My fan fare? Little fare
With which I buy my way, making things brave?
No, that is not it. Uncovering what is brave. The way
Now I bend over and with my foot turn up a stone,
And there they are: the armies of pale creatures who
Without cease or doubt sew the sweet sad earth.

Blacklegs

The sheep has nipples, the boy said,
And fur all around. The sheep
Has black legs, his name is Blacklegs,
And a cry like breaking glass.

The glass is broken. The glass
Is broken, and the milk falls down.

The bee has a suffering softness,
The boy said, a ring of fur,
Like a ring of fire. He burns
The flowers he enters, the way
The rain burns the grass. The bee
Has six legs, six strong legs,
And when he flies the legs
Whistle like a blade of grass
Brought to the lips and blown.

The boy said, The horse runs hard
As sorrow, or a storm, or a man
With a stolen purse in his shirt.
The horse's legs are a hundred
Or more, too many to count,
And he holds a moon white as fleece
In his mouth, cups it like water
So it will not spill out.

And the boy said this. I am a boy
And a man. My legs are two
And they shine black as the arrows
That drop down on my throat
And my chest to draw out the blood
The bright animals feed on,
Those with wings, those without,
The ghosts of the heart — whose
Hunger is a dress for my song.

Sheep Child

I wanted a child. What then, this? The sheep
Stands dumb behind the fence. Stands dumb.
Demanding what? Pity? Affection? A breast full
Of milk? He's up to his neck in his filthy fur.
Honey to the flies. Rancid honey. Each coarse
Curl dipped in it. The flies reeling. A sullen
Moment . . . Oh, Sheep, Sheep, this is my undoing:
That you have a thought and I would read it. I would
Put my head up to your smelly head and watch
The pretty pictures sliding past: Look! there goes
The flowerless larch, lurching over the ground
Like a skiff. And that black thing spinning in the dung
Is a truck tire stuffed with hay. And here, now,
Down from the elm, comes the crow, bully bird
Beating and beating the air with his wide wings
As if calling the field to order . . . There is no order.
What day of the week is this? Wash day?
Bake day? What hour of what day? . . . Behind you,
Flanked by steely thistle, stands the old goat,
Contemptuous, uninterested, gnawing on the last
Of a Sunday dress, and, "I had a goat once,"
The thought that comes to me, "I had a small
Black goat who pounded his head against a tree
Until he was dead. His name was Bumblee."
Well, night is coming on. No, it is dead afternoon.
But there is something about night in this cloud-
Shadowed field. Perhaps the stars are shifting
Behind the veil of day? Perhaps. Perhaps . . . Oh,
I would turn this pretty. You see the cowbirds,
Riding the bony heifer by the overturned bathtub?
The birds are dung-colored, yes, but when
They rise and swim together they change color,
Brown to red, the way the light changes color
At dusk. And yes, the swans by the back fence
Are foul-tempered and mean as sin, but look
How their necks wave about now like the stems

Of lilies in the wind . . . lilies blowing in the wind . . .
The goat snorts and turns his back. He has
Swallowed the last of the dress . . . Oh, Sheep, Sheep,
This is my undoing, that you have a thought
And I *can* read it. Dear Monstrous Child, I would
Nurse you if I could. But you are far too large.
And I am far too old for such foolishness.

The South Gate

Light cups the breasts of the lion. Who remains
Unbothered. Stone lion. Stained breasts suddenly
Full of milk. And no one to feed on them. No one
To catch the warm liquid as it falls, sweet and fast,
To the ground. Moss on the lion's legs. Moss
Bloodying her small feet. Moss darkening the fruit trees
Dressed now by the snow that raises the ghosts
Of dead flowers: A visible shadow: A touchable shadow:
Flesh of water and ash. Like the sun, the lion
Is a two-faced creature. One face looks forward.
The other back. One grins. The other grimaces.
Her four eyes are old. *Oh, it is a far far country*
The lion comes from. A place almost unimaginable,
So dull are we. The lion herself almost unimaginable,
Even with her curious form stationed above us.
Wide the arms of the roses nailed to the wall below her.
Dry the weeds. White the snow dressing the ground
And then dressing it no more. Low the sound
Where no sound should be, deep in the heart of the ground.
The lion will bear a child. How can a stone lion
Bear a living child? Because still in the corner
Of her deformed head a dream lodges. Her breasts
Produce milk. The sweet milk falls to the ground.
The ground is a flock of dead birds. The wind
Rises. The fed offspring stirs. Soon he will stagger
From burial. Terrible. Wrapped in soiled cloth.

Stinking. Lion flesh and bird flesh and man flesh.
We would prefer this were a trick. Strings
And ropes. But it is not. The lion will grow large.
The greenness is his hunger. His hunger will overtake
The ground and soon devour even the mother.
She will sleep in his belly. He will rock her softly.

Elegy

Wind buffs the waterstained stone cupids and shakes
Old rain from the pines' low branches, small change
Spilling over the graves the years have smashed
With a hammer — *forget this, forget that, leave no*
Stone unturned. The grass grows high, sweet-smelling,
Many-footed, ever-running. No one tends it. No
One comes . . . *And where am I now?* . . . Is this a beginning,
A middle, or an end? . . . Before I knew you I stood
In this place. Now I forsake the past as I knew it
To feed you into it. But that is not right. You *step*
Into it. I *find* you here, in the sifting grass,
In the late light, as if you had always been here.
Behind you two torn black cedars flame white
Against the darkening fields . . . If you turn to me,
Quiet man? If you turn? If I speak softly?
If I say, *Take off, take off your glasses . . . Let me see*
Your sightless eyes? . . . *I will be beautiful then* . . .
Look, the heart moves as the moths do, scuttering
Like a child's thoughts above this broken stone
And that. And I lie down. I lie down in the long grass,
Something I am not given to doing, and I feel
The weight of your hand on my belly, and the wind
Parts the grasses, and the distance spills through —
The glassy fields, the black black earth, the pale air
Streaming headlong toward the abbey's far stones
And streaming back again . . . The drowned scent of lilacs
By the abbey, it is a drug. It drives one senseless.

It drives one blind. You can cup the enormous lilac cones
In your hands — ripened, weightless, and taut —
And it is like holding someone's heart in your hands,
Or holding a cloud of moths. I lift them up, my hands.
Grave man, bend toward me. Lay your face . . . *here.*
Rest . . . I took the stalks of dead wisteria
From the glass jar propped against the open grave
And put in the shell-shaped yellow wildflowers
I picked along the road. I cannot name them.
Bread and butter, perhaps. I am not good
With names. But nameless you walked toward me
And I knew you, a swelling in the heart,
A silence in the heart, the wild wind-blown grass
Burning — as the sun falls below the earth —
Brighter than a bed of lilies struck by snow.

Sheet Music

If you cannot trust the dog, the faithful one?
And is this anyway a dog? The shadows move,
Dog and dog, two lanky figures, three, sniffing
The garden's charred terrain, the darkening grass

And bleeding beds of flowers, sniffing the stones
And lunging at the rabbits that spring from the beds,
Wet creatures, mad with haste, mad and wet
And white as the half-hearted moon that disappeared

Behind the clouds and has not yet come back . . . The rain
Fell hard, and now the mist rises, consolidates, disperses,
That thought, this, your face, mine, the shapes
Complicating the air in front of the abandoned birdhouse,

Big as a summer hotel, thirty rooms
For thirty birds, thirty perches from which to sing.

Such is the moon when it is full. A giant birdhouse
Tilted high on a steel pole, a pale blue box

Full of the shredded sheet music of long-dead birds . . .
The dogs move fast. How will I follow? And which one?
They are not in agreement. If the dog cannot be trusted?
Then what? The foot? But the foot is blind, the grass

Cold through the thin socks, the instep bared like a neck.
And now the flowers rise. The mums and asters,
The tall gladiolas knocked back by the rain creep up
In the mist; and the mist thickens and moves about me

Like a band of low-bred mummers, dripping scent,
Pulling my hair, my arms, trying to distract me;
But still I hear it, the dark sound that begins
At the edge of the mind, at the far edge of the uncut field

Beyond the garden — a low braying, donkey
Or wolf, a low insistent moan. If I whistle
Will the dogs come? Can I gather their trailing leashes
And hold them in my hand? They cannot be held.

How pale the paint of the birdhouse. How ghastly pale
The sound of the cry coming closer . . . If I forsake
The dogs? . . . If I forsake the mummers? . . . If I step
Like a fool into the glassy outer darkness? . . . *O self* . . .

Linear

When he looks at the others, I mean
When he not-looks at me,
That leaves me free
To memorize
The shirted shape for his back,
The sinuous lines throughout his hair,
Those, yes, and the rivery veins of his hands.

And when, on one of the nights,
It falls out that we walk back together,
It falls out that we descend into the formal garden,
It falls out that we take seats on respective ends of a bench,
I fall to measuring, think in shapes, in gradations:
Mountain, sky, their joinder in fog. Amazing,
The range of the night-grays.

We need a remark; I make it:
"Amazing, the range of grays at night.
Those shrubs look like granite, and the way they're spaced,
They make me think of tombstones."
"Yeah."
Mountain, sky . . .
"Yeah, it's strange." Joinder in fog . . .

The wine from the reception dizzies my faculties, his being here
Addles me, thrills me, to think, his heart
Beating under his shirt, my heart
Losing its grip, I
Glimpse —

I can't have seen that — bright return? not only against the rule
Against touch, untested, but against

A ban I already know
Intimately:
I'm not desirable.
I'm not prepared for desire.
If by night I feel a pull, by day I resay, it's delusion.
Then who is this actress, surfacing?
Speechless,

For if,
For even one second,
I 'part my lips,' if I tip
Towards him, even one inch, that inch
Could collapse the meter between us — second into instant — then
The face
Will be

Yanked away.
"Are you enjoying it here?"
I blink, I swallow, "Oh, yes!"
Swallowed kiss ≠ swallowed word;
Swallowed word ≠ swallowed tear;
Swallowed tear ≠ swallowed kiss.
Any 2 or all 3 may ensue at once.

But coincidence ≠ cause-&-effect.
Things to keep separate, straight.
He: "Well, I'm —
Pretty tired, should probably be finding my room."
Kept separate, kept straight. He continues, "Are you . . . ?"
"Oh, I think I'll stay here
A while."

"Well," he stands,
He has stood, he is taking a stand,
He has stood, he is going, I remember some lines I have learned:

If the lady and gentleman wish to take their tea in the garden,
If the lady and gentleman wish to take their tea in the garden . . .
"Yes, good night."
This is how

I can prevent calling his name out after him: Memorize,
Memorize his gait, his trousers, memorize
The four garden steps, he climbs,
Still noting the steps,
He's left,
Again note the shrubs.
Memorize the trapezoid roof of that

Shed, the studied, faceted lid of the gazebo,
Vertical pines, horizontal pine-shadows, stripes across ground.
Sky, fog, their joinder. Law
Despite the mountains.
I shut my eyes,
And on and on, the night-singing insects, those makers of round,
Keep on, and on . . .

I press my mouth, into my palm, hard,
And on, they sound. One form
Merging from myriad
Participants,
Seeming to know
When to come in, and when
To leave off, knowing start without cost, stop without halt.

Impetus

A man half Alan and half Uncle Arnold
Stopped by the millinery shop to mention:
"Cursed be any God who allows the old
To flop on this regular a basis." Shun

Any omnibus which is a tourists' tour,
Any present for the apparition of a Virgin
As in the Rinuccini Triptych's flames. Our
Tongues one by one by one by one cave in.

To get to the shop he went up a perpendicular
Road; the carriages had to be strapped to it.
He heard the dots in the park say, "No end
To this lot, they're all commonplace." I

Heard him say, "Right, but you err to be seeking
Minimal falls. Pastoral falls take flight:
You, Brook, release me, lift my weak king."
Back God comes, nailing horses' hooves to light.

Balm

The hip bone's connected to the (beat) thigh bone.
The thigh bone's connected to the (beat) knee bone.
The knee bone's connected to the (beat) shin bone.
Now hear the words of the Lord.

————————

I said to Laura,
"I don't see how novels can get written, they're so *long*."

"You just form a relationship with it," she said,
Tossing her Farrah-Fawcett hair,

"Like you do with your body, you know?
You do the things that are good for it,
Don't do the things that are bad for it, *you* know,
Like you can't *not* have a good relationship with
Your own body."

"Oh."

———————

First I slapped my face and chest
Until they were red and stinging.
Then I yanked from its hook in the bathroom
The pretty nightgown, the thin nightgown
With all those little tucks, the nightgown
Sprayed with Obsession perfume for a man
Who never showed. And I ripped it in two,
In four, in a dozen pieces, two dozen pieces —
How the pearl buttons flew!
Then I stabbed my hand with my pen —
This was during the loud groaning —
But the pen merely broke, so I took
And smeared the ink all over my tongue and
My cheeks, mixed in with the usual tears.
What a sight!
That's who I saw in the mirror then,
When I struck a match and lit the eyelet trim
On the yoke of her real nightgown,
The ugly flannel nightgown she had on
'That filthy girl on fire can't move!' and so
An invisible woman comes to her rescue,
Dashes, with cupped palms, water upon her.
And so they got to the dawn, rocking.
And got to a psychiatrist within the week.

———————

Now I wash every day, to remember.
I remember every day
With the clean white towel
And the almond-scented lotion:

The toe bone's connected to the (there) foot bone;
The foot bone's connected to the (there) ankle bone;
The ankle bone's connected to the (there) shin bone . . .
Now hear the

The comforting sound of crickets.

from *The Widening Spell of the Leaves*, "The Perfection of Solitude:
A Sequence"

2. Caravaggio: Swirl & Vortex

In the Borghese, Caravaggio, painter of boy whores, street punk, exile &
 murderer,
Left behind his own face in the decapitated, swollen, leaden-eyed head of
 Goliath,
And left the eyelids slightly open, & left on the face of David a look of pity

Mingling with disgust. A peach face; a death mask. If you look closely you can
 see
It is the same face, & the boy, murdering the man, is murdering his own
 boyhood,
His robe open & exposing a bare left shoulder. In 1603, it meant he was
 available,

For sale on the street where Ranuccio Tomassoni is falling, & Caravaggio,

Puzzled that a man would die so easily, turns & runs.

Wasn't it like this, after all? And this self-portrait, David holding him by a lock
Of hair? Couldn't it destroy time if he offered himself up like this, empurpled,
Bloated, the crime paid for in advance? To die before one dies, & keep
 painting?

This town, & that town, & exile? I stood there looking at it a long time.

A man whose only politics was rage. By 1970, tinted orchards & mass graves.

———————

The song that closed the Fillmore was "Johnny B. Goode," as Garcia played it,
Without regret, the doors closing forever & the whole Haight evacuated, as if
Waiting for the touch of the renovator, for the new boutiques that would
     open —

The patina of sunset glinting in the high, dark windows.

Once, I marched & linked arms with other exiles who wished to end a war,
     & . . .
Sometimes, walking in that crowd, I became the crowd, &, for that moment,
     it felt
Like entering the wide swirl & vortex of history. In the end,

Of course, you could either stay & get arrested, or else go home.

In the end, of course, the war finished without us in an empty row of horse
     stalls

Littered with clothing that had been confiscated.

_____

I had a friend in high school who looked like Caravaggio, or like Goliath —
Especially when he woke at dawn on someone's couch. (In early summer,
In California, half the senior class would skinny-dip & drink after midnight

In the unfinished suburb bordering the town, because, in the demonstration
     models,
They filled the pools before the houses sold . . . Above us, the lush stars
     thickened.)
Two years later, thinking he heard someone call his name, he strolled three
     yards

Off a path & stepped on a land mine.

_____

Time's sovereign. It rides the backs of names cut into marble. And to get
Back, one must descend, as if into a mass grave. All along the memorial, small
Offerings, letters, a bottle of bourbon, photographs, a joint of marijuana
    slipped

Into a wedding ring. You see, you must descend; it is one of the styles
Of Hell. And it takes a while to find the name you might be looking for; it is
Meant to take a while. You can touch the names, if you want to. You can kiss
    them,

You can try to tease out some final meaning with your lips.

The boy who was standing next to me said simply: "You can cry. . . . It's O.K.,
    here."

———————

"Whistlers," is what they called them. A doctor told me who'd worked the
    decks
Of a hospital ship anchored off Seoul. You could tell the ones who wouldn't
    last
By the sound, sometimes high-pitched as a coach's whistle, the wind made
    going

Through them. I didn't believe him at first, & so then he went into greater
Detail . . . Some evenings, after there had been heavy casualties & a brisk
    wind,
He'd stare off a moment & think of a farm in Nebraska, of the way wheat

Bent in the wind below a slight rise, & no one around for miles. All he wanted,
He told me, after working in such close quarters for twelve hours, for sixteen
Hours, was that sudden sensation of spaciousness — wind, & no one there.

My friend, Zamora, used to chug warm vodka from the bottle, then execute a
    perfect
Reverse one-&-a-half gainer from the high board into the water. Sometimes,
When I think of him, I get confused. Someone is calling to him, & then

• • •

I'm actually thinking of Caravaggio . . . in his painting. I want to go up to it

And close both the eyelids. They are still half open & it seems a little obscene

To leave them like that.

7. Coda: Kind of Blue

And *So what?* said a trumpet; & *I'll see you that & raise you five,* said a kind
Of rippling laughter, gone now, on the keyboard; & *Well just this once,* the bass
Replied; *Maybe again, maybe not,* a brush stroke swore on a snare & high hat. Styles

As American as loss: *I'm going to say what the snow says, falling on the tracks
Outside Chicago, & then I'll unsay that. I'll dissolve this city, wall by blackened
Wall, & Mr. Grief & Ms. Beauty, I'll build a new one from your names.* Ashes,

> My name is Mr. John Coltrane,
> Sweet insolence, & rain.
> I don't come back again.

And *Am I Blue? So What? You think I didn't know what time it was?* said the trumpet.
Take her hair, some smoke & snow, & give it all one name. Style it as you please.
Take someone who can't stop screaming, the el overhead, the sky, & give it a name.

Take Charlie Parker's grave all overgrown with weeds in Kansas City. Add nothing,
Except an ocher tint of shame. May all your Christmases be white & Bird be still
In L.A., gone, broken, insane. Take Beauty before her habit mutes & cripples her,

. . .

Then add some grief. But don't change a thing this time, not even a white
  gardenia
Pressed against her ear. Not even one syllable of her name. "In my solitude"
Is how the song began. All things you are, & briefly, as, in solitude, it ends.

Portrait

Purblind, he rose, shot his cuffs, and hit
the door, a gangster
but gangless, dead in the heart, dead
in the rat-black rumdum redundant heart, lost
to this world and not RSVPing
invites to the next.
Is this the one who would lead us to a new aesthetic?
Is this the one, fragile, moribund, afraid,
will lead the fragile, moribund, and afraid?
Is this the New Truth messenger,
the one who will define
the New Politics
or the New Poetics
with the Old Oblique?
His famous sneer eats his gut like a worm.

Beauty School

On the Avenue of Fashion,
in the noted necropolis, kitty corner
from a croissant shop
and four blocks down
from a dozen banks
is the campus of the Beauty School,
where we learn to walk
assuming we are watched
and where, somewhere, in each book
is placed a mirror: *Lost in books,*

we say, late for a study break
date, *I got lost*
in the text. The teacher
stands at the front
of the room: he's the teacher.
The students sit in rows,
those with cheaper haircuts in the rear.
The class is Aesthetics 101.
Beauty is everywhere, the teacher says,
tossing its head.
And when we graduate
the world is there for us, whole, to dread,
to drain.

Henry Clay's Mouth

Senator, statesman, Speaker of the House,
exceptional dancer, slim,
graceful, ugly. Proclaimed, before most, slavery
an evil, broker
of elections (burned Jackson
for Adams), took a pistol ball in the thigh
in a duel, delayed, by forty years,
with his compromises, the Civil War,
gambler ("I have always
paid peculiar homage to the fickle goddess."),
booze hound, ladies' man — which leads us
to his mouth, which was huge,
a long slash across his face,
with which he ate and prodigiously drank,
with which he modulated his melodic voice,
with which he liked to kiss and kiss and kiss.
He said: "Kissing is like the presidency,
it is not to be sought and not to be *declined*."
A rival, one who wanted to kiss
whom he was kissing, said: "The ample

dimensions of his kissing apparatus
enabled him to *rest* one side of it
while the other was on active duty."
If women had the vote,
it was written, if women had the vote,
he would have been president,
kissing everyone in sight,
dancing on tables ("a grand Terpsichorean
performance . . ."), kissing everyone,
sometimes two at once, kissing everyone,
the almost-president
of our people.

Tactile

One eyelash, one
millimeter
longer than each other eyelash on your left eyelid, bends
at its tip, as it, alone, leans
on my lowest left rib's ledge, this single filament
holding your bones
to mine. A touch of no touch, a touch
so light the tactile scale's
needle barely breathes. Then,
attached to an human as it is,
this one eyelash
lashes me there, many times,
and tonight the tiny scars
shine in the blue-stone dark.

Pre-Cerebral

for Cecilia

No ideas. No thoughts, nor
philosophy. Hunger, thirst,
yes, flight and fear. And touch, sound,
and sight, and the tongue, which tastes.
Ten fingers, the heart's in place.
Two arms, legs, esophagus.
Looking down: that's the sweet ground.
Looking up: that's the wide sky.
Miles after miles, the wide sky.
And touch. And the tongue, which tastes.

Bonehead

Bonehead time, bonehead town. Bonehead teachers.
Bonehead mom, bonehead dad, bonehead aunts
and uncles and cousins too.
Bonehead me, bonehead you.
Bonehead books, playground, box lunch, fast food,
tract homes, Sunday school.
Bonehead Truman, McCarthy, Eisenhower too.
Bonehead me, bonehead you.
Bonehead music, TV, H-bomb, movies,
butch-cut, tail fins, baby boom.
Bonehead Russia, America, England too.
Bonehead me, bonehead you.

The Orange

Gone to swim after walking the boys to school.
Overcast morning, mid-week, off-season,
few souls to brave the warm, storm-tossed waves,
not wild but rough for this tranquil coast.

Swimming now. In rhythm, arm over arm,
let the ocean buoy the body and the legs work little,
wave overhead, crash and roll with it, breathe,
stretch and build, windmill, climb the foam. Breathe,

breathe. Traveling downwind I make good time
and spot the marker by which I know to halt
and forge my way ashore. Who am I
to question the current? Surely this is peace abiding.

Walking back along the beach I mark the signs of erosion,
bide the usual flotsam of seagrass and fan coral,
a float from somebody's fishing boat,
crusted with sponge and barnacles, and then I find

the orange. Single irradiant sphere on the sand,
tide-washed, glistening as if new born,
golden orb, miraculous ur-fruit,
in all that sweep of horizon the only point of color.

Cross-legged on my towel I let the juice course
and mingle with the film of salt on my lips
and the sand in my beard as I steadily peel and eat it.
Considering the ancient lineage of this fruit,

• • •

the long history of its dispersal around the globe
on currents of animal and human migration,
and in light of the importance of the citrus industry
to the state of Florida, I will not claim

it was the best and sweetest orange in the world,
though it was, o great salt water
of eternity,
o strange and bountiful orchard.

Because This Is Florida

Because this is Florida, we can be what we choose to be,
say, Dixie-fried Cubano rednecks. It's that kind of place.
When the heavy metal band plays "Rocky Top, Tennessee"

they all stomp and sing along — I should say *we*
sing along, at the annual State Fair, a very weird place.
Because this is Florida, I feel like an anomaly,

but the truth of it is I'm them and they're me,
and now we're stamping and hooting all over the place
while the Texas swing band plays "Rocky Top, Tennessee"

and Haitian kids dip kettle candy beneath a live oak tree
in historic *Cracker Country,* apt and ironic misnomer for the place,
because this is Florida, after all, not Texas or Tennessee.

Florida, Florida. At times I can't believe what I see
and don't know how to feel about living in a place
where a bluegrass fiddler plays "Rocky Top, Tennessee"

while Rome burns. Is it just me, or an epidemic of mistaken identity,
the state of confusion that plagues this sun-bedeviled place?
Because this is Florida, I beg you to believe me,
the steel drum band from Trinidad plays "Rocky Top, Tennessee."

The Zebra Longwing

Forty years I've waited,
uncomprehending,
for these winter nights
when the butterflies
fold themselves like paper cranes
to sleep in the dangling
roots of the orchids
boxed and hung
from the live oak tree.
How many there are.
Six. Eight. Eleven.
When I mist the spikes
and blossoms by moonlight
they stir but do not wake,
antennaed and dreaming
of passionflower
nectar. Never before
have they gifted us
in like manner, never before
have they stilled their flight
in our garden. Wings
have borne them away
from the silk
of the past as surely
as some merciful wind
has delivered us
to an anchorage of such
abundant grace,
Elizabeth. All my life
I have searched, without knowing it,
for this moment.

Benediction for the Savior of Orlando

Signs and wonders: *Jesus Is Lord Over Greater Orlando*
snake-tagged in cadmium on a vine-grown cyclone
fence along I-4 southbound north of downtown
is a credo that subverts the conventional wisdom
that Walt Disney is the messiah and his minions the christened
stewards of this place, that the Kingdom to Come shall be Mickey's,
that the bread of our communion will be proffered by A.T.M.
and the wine quaffed without taint of sulfites
or trademark infringement, all of which is certainly true
and yet too pat, too much like shooting mice in a barrel
when there are nastier vermin to contest
and purgatories far worse than Disney's realm of immortal
simulacra suckled at the breast of Lake Buena Vista.
There is, for one, Orlando itself,
Orlando rightly considered, Orlando qua Orlando.
Nobody, anywhere, could honestly propose Orlando
as a fit model for human habitation,
city with the character of a turnpike restroom,
city with the soul of a fastfood establishment,
sanitized and corporatized, homogenous and formulaic.
Orlando is the holy land of the branded and franchised,
Orlando is the Jerusalem of commodified delight,
Orlando, Orlando, so many Orlandos
I commence to feel downright Shakespearean,
but here is no Rosalind to dignify our tale,
no Touchstone to transform its tragedy to farce,
because Orlando is the Florida I fear to conceive,
Florida ordained like the ante-chamber to that afterworld
where jackal-headed Anubis prepares his embalmer's instruments
to pump our veins with tincture of liquid sunshine
until we are reduced to somnambulant acquiescence,
a citizenry mummified within the cambric of material satiety,
within the gated stucco walls of economic segregation
and the hairy stucco arms of Armed Response security,
a people determined to rev our outboards and troll for bass
in the shadow of the form-glass temples to corporate profit

while the fill ponds grow heavy with duckweed and algae
and the golf courses burn with viridian fire
through seasons of rain and seasons of drought
and the metropolis spreads ever outward the bland picnic blankets
of its asphalt dominion, landscape drained of spontaneity and glee,
bones boiled free of communal gristle — is it any wonder
the children of this America rise up with guns
to wreak a senseless vengeance,
the very children that might have saved us,
the ones we had relied on to assemble in fellowship
and attend to councils of greater wisdom
than those to which we have given credence?
Perhaps the children were absent from school
the day these lessons were offered or perhaps
the lessons have been censored from the curriculum
or there was no curriculum or the schools
had been demolished to make room for the future,
a serial cataclysm of vinyl and asphalt,
a republic of bananas and Banana Republics,
where cars are the chosen and credit cards the elect,
where Judge Judy balances the Scales of Justice
and the anthem of our freedom is sung by Chuck E. Cheese.
Here I may testify with absolute conviction:
Chuck E. Cheese is the monstrous embodiment of a nightmare,
the bewhiskered Mephistopheles of ring toss,
the vampire of our transcendent ideals.
Every Chuck E. Cheese's erected across the mall-lands of America
is another nail in the coffin of human aspiration
and every hour spent in one takes six months off your life.
No, no, no, it's not a theme restaurant or family amusement center
but a vision of infernal despair enjoined in plastic flames,
the clownish horror of the place is unspeakable,
yet I feel that I must speak of it, for I have been
to the birthday party of Emily, turning five,
the birthday party of Max, turning eight or nine,
of Max again, of David and Doris, of Myrna and Roberto,
I can bear witness to its odors of chocolate milk and floor cleanser,
the formica falsity of its processed cheesefood pseudo-pizza,

its banquet tables arrayed with pitchers of lurid orange soda
and the kids in the arcade room playing air hockey
and whack-a-mole and teaching one another to cheat at skiball
to win a screel of coupons to redeem for tiny, chintzy prizes,
the worst sorts of craftily packaged trash —
stringless army parachute guys, malformed monster finger puppets,
Chinese yoyos that self-destruct at the flip of a wrist —
a rainbow-colored peepshow designed to entice the youngest among us
to invest their lives in a cycle of competitive consumption
and then the animatronic hoedown commences its banjo jangle,
the hairy rodent orchestra chirring their cymbals on stage
as the gray rat-man emerges from his curtain redolent of mildew,
the incubus, the secret sharer, Chuck E. Cheese himself,
and the baby children scream in dismay and the larger children
gag with disinterest and the parents pay no attention at all
while employees with the fear- and candy-glazed eyeballs
of medium-security inmates stutter their pre-scripted remarks
over a public address system in whose interstitial silences
one may discern the voices of the lost upraised in prayer.

We're having a great day at Chuck E. Cheese —
   Hear us, help us, grant us benison,
Pick up your food at the counter PJ —
   Comfort and guide us, lead us to salvation,
Everyone loves family fun at Chuck E. —
   Bestow the mercies of your blessing
Cheese for your safety wear shoes at all times —
   Upon our souls, we beseech Thee,
Last call for pickup PJ last call —
   Lord of our fathers, almighty God.

Past All Understanding

The langouste's long feelers may be the result of a single gush of thought. — Ezra Pound

For it is the opinion of choice virtuosi that the brain is only a crowd of little animals,
but with teeth and claws extremely sharp. — Jonathan Swift

A woman there was balancing her baby
back-to-back. They held each other's hands and did
a kind of teeter-totter on each other's inclinations,
making casual covalency into
a human ideogram,
spontaneous Pilobolus —
a spectacle at which
the estimable Kooch
(half Border and half Lab)

began to bark. He wouldn't stop. The child slid off
the woman's back — now they were two again, and so
he quieted a bit. But they were two who scowled
and stared (now it was I who grew disquieted). You looked,
I started to explain, like one

big oddity to him. (They weren't appeased.) He barks
at crippled people too. (Now they were horrified.)
Meanwhile a wind

rose at the kiosk, stapled with yard-jobs, sub-clubs, bands somebody named
for animals. The whole park seemed to flutter up and flail, and Kooch,
unquenchable, perceived the higher truth. Its upshot was a bout of barking
as to make the bicyclists bypassing (bent beneath their packs),
an assortment of teaching assistants (harried, earnest, hardly earning),

and even the white-haired full professorships all come to a halt, in the wake
of the waves of their tracks. What brouhahas! What flaps! To Kooch's mind,

if you could call it that,
the worst was yet to come —

for looming overhead a host of red
and yellow kites appeared, intent on swooping
even to the cowlicks of the humans — Were these people blind? —
that woman in pink, that man in blue, who paused there in his purview,
stupidly, to shake their heads? He thinks

we're in danger, I tried again
to reason with my fellow man. But now the dog
was past all understanding; he was uncontainable. He burst
into a pure fur paroxysm, blaming the sky for all
that we were worth: he held his ground
with four feet braced

against the overturning earth . . .

The Looker

I was as dead as I could be, and you
weren't there. They held a big glass
up to me; they blocked the world with
their lifelonging. What they wanted was

a cloud (the kind that tells the living of
themselves). But I was well past telling.
I was a looker at last, head back, mouth wide
as in a heat or holler. (I had always looked my best

. . .

in song or some astonishment. With a nose as close
to her chin as this, what aesthete would be caught dead
with her mouth shut? It's a matter of the golden mean.
And yet she knows — who cannot shut her mouth —

she'd better be of finest words, and few. A matter of
the golden rule. A kind of courtesy. No faking, no
mistaking. Only real love-moans, or wonders un-
translatable.) No sweat. When you're as dead as this,

you're not a cheat or chatterbox. Don't fear to look.
Don't look to stay. Given the almost-clear, the near-
unclouded glass, in your absence I did what I could:
I took my breath away.

Etymological Dirge

'Twas grace that taught my heart to fear.

Calm comes from burning.
Tall comes from fast.
Comely doesn't come from come.
Person comes from mask.

The kin of charity is whore.
The root of charity is dear.
Incentive has its source in song
And winning in the sufferer.

Afford yourself what you can carry out.
A coward and a coda share a word.
We get our ugliness from fear.
We get our danger from the lord.

What He Thought

We were supposed to do a job in Italy
and, full of our feeling for
ourselves, being the Poets
from America, we went
from Rome to Fano, met
the mayor, did the photo-shoots
and thanked the flowergirls before we mulled

a couple matters over, from the dais: "What's
a cheap date?" someone asked us. "What's
a flat drink?" There, among Italian literati,
we could recognize our counterparts:
the academic, the apologist,
the arrogant, the amorous,
the brazen and the glib.
And there was one

administrator (the conservative), in suit
of regulation gray, who like a good tour guide
with measured pace and uninflected tone
narrated sights and histories the hired van
hauled us past. Of all he was most politic and least
poetic, so it seemed. Our last few days in Rome, when all
but three of the New World Bards had flown, I found

a book of poems this unprepossessing one had written: it had lain
unnoticed in the pensione room (a room he'd recommended)
where it must have been abandoned by the German visitor
— (was there a bus of them?) — to whom
he had inscribed and dated it a month before.
I couldn't read Italian either, so I shoved it back into
the wardrobe's dark.
                            We last Americans were due
to leave tomorrow. For our parting evening then, our host chose
something in a family restaurant, and there we sat and chatted, sat
and chewed, till — sensible it was our last big chance to

be poetic, make our mark, one of us asked

                    "What's

poetry? Is it the fruits and vegetables
and marketplace of Campo dei Fiori, or
the statue there?" Because I was

the glib one, I identified the answer instantly,
I didn't have to think — "The truth
is both, it's both!" I blurted out.
But that was easy. That
was easiest to say.
What followed

taught me something about difficulty,
for our underestimated host spoke out, all
of a sudden, with a rising passion, and he said:

The statue represents Giordano Bruno,
brought to be burned in the public square
because of his offense against authority, which was
to say the Church. His crime was his belief
the Universe does not revolve around the human being;
God is no fixed point, or central government, but rather is
poured in waves through all things. All things move. "If God is not
the soul itself, He is the soul of the soul of the world." Such was his heresy.

The day they brought him forth to die, they feared he might
incite the crowd (the man was famous for
his eloquence). And so his captors
placed upon his face
an iron mask
in which he could not speak.

That's how they burned him. That is how
he died, without a word, in front
of everyone.
                    And poetry —

                        (we'd all
put down our forks by now, to listen to
the man in gray; he went on
softly) —
              poetry is what

he thought but did not say.

Just Some

Monday minus sex, man in the air, mom
in the moon-milk, God, your zip code
keeps eluding me. Oh one,
oh one, oh one.
Hexagonad, you're pent up plus.
You aren't most numb,
like any bombast gas's additive —
your metric is comparatively
uncontainable, your come
all emanations, weep all throes.
Spare us, spare us a sea,
spare us a sec. Our
weather is what
your will wasn't —
ever (over and over) to be.

Havana Dream

The red eye blinks and it is you
(in between the rain)

out of the crumbling rooms,
a note played on the piano,

a salt wind off the ocean,
lonely, refracted (you).

Amor Vincit Omnia

So this is where the cunning
coney lives.

Look at it come close, go far,
cross highways, reach the sea,

its ambidextrous eyes
leaping (perpendicular) like fish.

Venus in Varadero

The sea is chaste with many minds.
One is naked (she walks

out of the waves). Another
invented silence (her hair becomes

the wind). The third remembers
the music (before she was a song).

The Peasant Heart

At dusk the snow turns blue,
the moon yawns to frigid black.

And you? Bone long
and deep to the south.

I wanted song (return).
I had the knowledge of never.

Before the Solutions

In the boxes a year's supply
of moods (bovine, sublunary).

I hear them out,
I hear them in.

New tone on the street,
new tone, same boxes.

End of the Affair

Funny how the fun collapses,
archaic, blended into threnody.

Funny how we dream of hoping
and go back to the books,

the dusty shelves. (Funny how)
our patience lapses.

Butterflies That Save Us from Ourselves

It came in pills, the mescaline, very fat, imposing, translucent capsules,
And inside, the blue powder which promised, Jon said,
To revert us to our true characters, then went into the bathroom
With a pile of books, ran the water, and lay in the tub,
Calling out every once in a while, *How's everybody doing?* Gail
Disappeared down the corridor. Linda in the parlor
Stripped off her blouse exposing big round nipples that seemed,
As the drug began to take effect, to be growing larger and darker —
Wine-stains on a white bed-sheet, I thought. Skin like luminescent ice,
And underneath, the blue streams, and in them the red fingerlings
Swimming, I thought, toward the source. The source! But what was it?
Our characters, Jon had said. *Who are we?* I asked Linda,
And she said, *Take off your clothes*, which I did, and we started playing
    doctor —
Not sex, but she said *Let's look at our bodies close up,*
And when I got a hard-on she said, *Let's meditate.*
That's when I heard the noise. A terrible sobbing, then a deep
Replenishing breath, more sobbing, and whether it was emanating
From inside me, or outside, I couldn't be sure, so floated down the corridor,
Feeling *beside myself,* and on the journey some of the bad things
That had happened to me and the bad things I had promulgated onto others
Were riffing through my brain like speeded-up scenes
In a Laurel and Hardy short. My father in his striped pajamas yelling.
My mother on the sofa darning socks, moving her mouth
The way she used to, but no words. A woman walking toward me
And a woman walking away, different women then the same,
And through it all the same one-note song, *I hate myself.*
Then there she was, Gail, curled up on the bed. *What's the matter?* I asked.
I have no pockets to put my thoughts in! —

Then I was stroking her hair, trying to make nice like a child will
With a traumatized adult, watching the bad thoughts
Spasm across her face. Then Jon was turning the thin pages
Of a book of Japanese water colors. Translucent and pale
And layered. The land moving up and the land moving down,
Whiskered with clouds, and scattering here and there
Specks that could have been people or could have been butterflies,·
And I thought, or I said: *This is as long ago as long ago gets.*
And sure enough it seemed to take hours, this viewing,
As though we'd all our lives been looking at these pictures.
This was our country and they were our landscape. Jon would always be
Subtly altering the landscape because that was his job. Gail
Would always be crying, but more softly now,
And we would linger there forever, somewhere in the sixties,
Out of the weather of time and before we reverted
From our true characters to the rest of our true lives.

Reverie: *The Saturday Evening Post*

Age ten, I wanted to write those sentimental stories that made me cry,
Historical stories I read in *The Saturday Evening Post*
While sitting in the big blue chair next to the Philco radio. Historical
Because written in what I was learning was the past tense,
Meaning something had already occurred; sentimental
Because a person could go on with life, a little bit chastened, a little bit wiser,
After the story's end.
                    The Saturday Evening Post made me cry once a week,
So I wanted to make everyone in the neighborhood cry
Each time they saw a full moon bulging at the horizon,
Or smelled new-mown hay on a Sunday drive,
As my father used to do, out on the washboard dirt roads
Where people lived far enough apart to feel independent,
My father used to say, yet close enough to know
When an old man died or a baby was born or two young people
Walked hand in hand at the end of the story.

Even my father, a skeptical man who didn't believe in God,
Who believed that work was the only salvation —
Like all the fathers, insensitive, thoughtless, now that I look back on them —
Who was slowly going blind from what I imagined
Was a speck of rot in his eye, would cry
When I sat in his lap and read him a story,
Or we listened to *One Man's Family*. We cried
Whenever something sad happened and sometimes even at the happy
    moments.

I don't remember a single story from the *Post*. They were written
Only to give you that burning pinch behind the eyes
And make you, at the end, feel good about your life
Because that was the only one you had. When you finished,
That week's issue got bundled in with the week's newspapers
And when you got a bunch of stacks
You gave them to the Boy Scouts or the YMCA paper drive.

Everything was different, of course, in 1952.
People rarely cursed, and when they did they made the sign of the cross
And were immediately forgiven. And the closest a grown-up came
To talking about sex was when my aunt once said, *The only thing I hate*
About being pregnant is everyone knows what you did.
And time was different, too. All day Saturday the neighbor's son
Would polish with a chamois cloth
The shapely silver gas tank of his *Springfield* motorcycle
Until it shone, and in it, mirrored, you could see my house
With its tall screened windows, and my mother inside, ironing or baking
Or polishing the silverware. There were paper routes. It snowed
More than it snows now. If a boy got in trouble he joined the service
And when he came back he was quiet and strong —
The next day he'd be standing in line
With his lunch bucket waiting for the bus with the other men.

And no one spoke about the war, or about the last hours of Mr. and Mrs.
    Healey,
Or what the yelling was about behind closed doors, or why the Smith boy,
Who had the squashed features of an Asian monkey

And who used to sit all day rocking on his porch,
Suddenly wasn't there. *I wonder what happened to dumb Jimmy,*
My father asked one day, and that was it. Jimmy was part of the story.
He had already happened and then the next thing would happen,
While out the window the neighborhood spun its leaves
From one season to the next, the snow got shoveled and the lilacs burst,
People went away and usually came back, and those who didn't
Were still part of the story, except they were history.

Even now, when the dumb god, *Change,* musters his ragged army
Every morning and marches them through the streets of the neighborhoods,
I'm still a nostalgic man. History cures nothing.
Irony? Perspective? Nothing. *The past,*
As Delmore Schwartz said, *is inevitable.* It sits in its big blue chair
Turning the pages of the *Post,* stopping at the jokes
Any innocent could understand, at the ads for TV's
People were beginning to buy because the times were good,
Every father had a job, everything glossy and in black and white.

Now, when even the past itself is going blind, hardening and blurring
At the peripheries, I have a soft spot for those naps after supper,
Sitting in my father's lap, as he was slowly going blind
And before he lost his job, as I rose and fell
With his unlabored breathing, evenings I wanted to write about
For the *Post* because they had already happened
And because we were all sure they would happen again.

Nature Rarely Confides in Me

The pomegranates slicken after a rain. I know what color they are, exactly,
Because I once had a magenta 300cc Honda motorcycle that glistened
In daylight and dimmed at night, like these pomegranates.
The birds love them and peck at them.
Then one drops, a pomegranate,
Somehow both slowly and suddenly,
And if you're lucky — which I am —

You're sitting on a hard slatted bench in the yard one evening after supper,
Learning how to sit and see.
Why are you so argumentative? my wife had said.
Why don't you go out in the yard and stare at the pomegranates
Before we get into a fight.
I looked up the spelling, first.
                                    I had a girlfriend in 1964 I've never forgotten.
Excuse me, but here in the yard I can still see the color of her nipples
And her black pubic hair curling up from her pale white skin,
And the splatter of cum on her thighs.
I wonder if it's raining where she is? Then I wonder
If she's bending over a sink, doing the supper dishes
Like my wife is and I wonder if
She still wears that perfume that smelled like lilacs after a rain.

The past: that's what I think about while meditating on the pomegranates.
That's when the trouble always starts. The past is all we've got
When we haven't yet learned how to sit and see.

If you've never seen a pomegranate, the insides are packed
With sections of luscious-looking seeds
Separated by yellowish membranes,
For some reason Nature has yet to confide in me.
If you put one on a plate and peel back the thick rind
And dig out a few gelatinous seeds, they taste sweet and wet,
Though dry, like wine.
I'm learning how to taste, too.
It has something to do with paying attention
To the wet slick walls of your mouth,
The way you can taste certain words in foreign languages.
My wife says, *Eat slower, you'll figure it out.*
                                    My mind tries to sit still,
But it won't, like this poem that wants to be about pomegranates
Because they have their own incomparable, lumpy, asymmetrical beauty,
Nothing like a woman's or a motorcycle's.
                                    When I was younger
I used to whiz through the dawn on my way home
From the *Wall Street Journal* printing plant
Where I worked the graveyard shift, proofreading.

I'd pick up my girlfriend and we had a secret spot to go make love,
A blackberry bramble some kids had made tunnels through.
We did it so often it made her sore. We did it so much she cried out once,
This is not natural!

      Back then, back east, there were no pomegranates
To instruct me in color, so the lady at the Motor Vehicle Registry
Followed me out to the curb and said,
It's colored magenta. And, *That's some*
Pretty machine for a boy to own.
All that night I corrected *The Wall Street Journal.*
If I saw the word *magenta*, I'd have recognized it.
If I'd have seen the word *pomegranate,*
I'd have been impelled to look it up.
Back then, words were everything to me.
That's when the trouble always started.
My girlfriend would say, *Why don't we take a walk instead?*
And I would say something like, *If you say the word* walk *seven times*
You'll sound like a crow by the side of the road. Tonight I'd say,
Did you know that different languages have different onomatopoeia
For different bird songs?

      So far only one pomegranate has fallen,
And it's dark by now, and if I were a Chinese poet instead of an American poet
I'd be satisfied. Maybe I'd want to go into the house and hear my wife say,
What did you see? Did you learn anything? And I would say,
Nature rarely confides in me. Or I might say,
To travel well is better than to arrive.
And my wife might say back to me,
On a withered branch a crow is perched
In the autumn evening,
And be satisfied.

      Before dawn, I used to whiz through the dark, slick streets,
My mind full of sex, my mouth full of words like *World Bank*
And *Gross National Product.* One infamous poet, on his deathbed,
Said something like, *I died of too many words.*
And my wife,
A practical woman I love
Sometimes even more than words, says, *You think too much,*
And, *Be careful of that shirt. The stains are so hard to get out.*

Bolt from the Blue: A Sequence

1. Bolt from the Blue

Gash in the azure
fabric —

Lightning crack
of ravish.
What's touched
is trashed —
ash and blast.

To rip the sky
then vanish.

Tatterflag
I raise —
shredded blue
above
dazed battlements.

2. Struck

To die and yet
live after —

how hide
that shatter?

what mask
of bold
or blank to wear?

3. Celestial Desolations

Zigzag nerve zap —
harsh torch-touch
that scorched
like a skim of frost,
turned bones
to smoke — it
scarred the heart most.

Can't halt what starts
from that marring —

jarred into knowledge
of gist and pith,
crux and thrust,
it keeps
a tight grip;
neither weaker
nor stronger,
but wiser, harder.

4. Elemental Scar

First choice —
to nurse
or spurn
the hurt?

Second,
how live
with all
the soft
parts
burned away?

Bare tree
branded
on the heart —

dry twigs
and wizening.

Neither sun
nor rain
assists —
to grow
at all
is to grow
slowly:
to force
the petals,
to *will*
the buds to leaf.

5. The Dance

That lightning stroke —
a rainbow bolt —
tore right through you
and is already
speeding past the stars.

All this you see —
dance of dazzle
and debris — is aftermath.

(Trauma) Storm

Hunkered down, nerve-numb,
in the carnal hut,
the cave of self
while outside a storm
rages.
          Huddled there,
rubbing together

white sticks of
your own ribs,
praying for sparks
in that dark
where tinder is heart,
where tender is not.

Screaming Out Loud

Before, you curled inward
around hurts and scars;
braille of battles
seldom won; fissures
and wristroads
a razor made.
           Stutter
from tongue-stump
unable to utter
its woe.
         Still,
your body was mostly
intact, and you
told yourself:
I'm a lucky husk.

And now, you're shattered,
hurtled outward:
shrapnel of stars
and a weird music:
bone in the wind's throat.

Almost a Loneliness

One and by one
we come to this place.
And those with companions
are also alone.

Sky and earth
and all the world
before us.

It's possible
to imagine the tree,
standing by itself.

But also the flowers —
how the weight
of so much being
bows them down.

How Smoothly . . .

How smoothly time moves
from moment to moment
without a pause,
without even
an eddy in its flow.

You'd think death
might slow it briefly.
You'd think this hole
in the earth
and this carved
stone might
swirl or flurry it.

. . .

Good-bye, little boat
going out
on the dark water.
Good-bye, little leaf
on the wide stream.

Be-All

The insect clings
to the green
stalk, sucks
its sap,
holds to the world
because it knows
the world is whole
and holy — the be-all
and the end-all
of it.
      But me —
I feel I'm ghost
and gristle
both.
      My sickness
is to think
there's something
out there called
the Infinite —

a place where
all my longing
will become *belong*.

Ovidian

Who stares into a wood and sees a dress fastened to a tree
recalls the torso of a man with arms held up among the wrens
and desires the man. Who moves among desires understands
stasis is the harder art. What feels like one is often two,
as how eyes look, or more than two, as how sunset opposes
noon, or how desire abides in memory, roving where
a girl in woods unfastens her sundress, a tree suspends
a flock, wrens flutter in a girl, a torso gently aches
inside a tree. The eye wants something other than it sees,
and what it sees. A hem lifts in the leaves.

Confession 1.8.13

Passing through innocence, I came either to experience
or guilt, or they came to me, displacing innocence,
which didn't leave (where would it have gone),
and yet it was no more. I was no longer
an unmarked girl but a woman gesturing.
It was not that the world showed itself to me
in a set method. Longing in stillnesses
and various tendencies of thought, I thought to be touched
by the world as it willed, or by whoever knew me.
I did myself, by the understandings objects gave me,
practice this touching, this being touched.
When things said themselves, and saying, sang,
I listened and imagined they themselves were presences
of stillnesses and movements, a music visible.
That they meant themselves and no others was plain

from shapes they took as leaves or men or rain. And so
by my constant thoughts on shapes as they appeared,
I collected what they stood for, and having broken in
my body to these signs, I gave gestures of opening to it.

Confession 10.8.13

Collect and recollect. These things I do
within, where, present with me is the world
and whatever I could think of it,
and what I have forgotten. Some things
I buried, though they seemed self-buried,
or slipped out of my mind when they had
glided further into me as I believed
them gone. Once my mouth had been aroused
by the side of a man's thumb moving over it,
the image fixed in me by that impress
recalls the hand, or my heightening,
as if I know my lover when I have him,
or when I have no one. In this way
my mind contains my body and can keep
in mind delight, whether I revisit with the
pleasure of my body, or I revisit thinking
my sad thoughts, or I keep back my desire
like the broken animals.

Confession 4.2.3

In hope of loving what is real
and in hope of being loved
by something real, believing that my mind
is intermingled with what is done by me,
what is the seeing of a snake in the rope
except hallucination, and what else is the seeing

of a deer on the path when there is
no deer there? When I feed the wind
with thinking and longing, am I the pleasure
of nothing? I have not seen a vivid wind,
and trying caused my eyes to close
and I saw nothing, no differently
than when I fall asleep. Mornings I know
the mirror that reflects my face
reflected first its maker as all mirrors do,
and returns me a reversal of myself.
How will I recognize the secret shapes
of my accompaniment, and what word would I say?

Two Sisters

There they are before desire went to them,
one preferring spring, when the smaller shapes
seem really willing to be seen, one preferring fall
for the yellow heaviness dragging over over-ripeness,
opening it before it leaves. These two are children.
One knows to sleep on top the other, fitting her cheek
against her thigh with a turned-out head,
knees hooked over the farther thigh, a ladle and tureen.
From her shoulders to her hips the smaller body crosses
her sister's open legs. The larger one has looked
at how she's crossed to magnify the feeling, and she'll
look again. She loves the spring. Her sister floats under
the arm draped over her and the cupped hand roving
her sleepy sleepy head where something opens and
divides and illustrates, divides and wants reverberation,
wants the floaty feeling after being touched by form,
then formlessness. She loves the fall.

Confession 2.5.10

What is the joy of the moral heart
if the great secret of morals is love,
if my heart, trying its nature,
makes a mirror of itself
for a body not my own,
if my heart is returned to me
as a body of water will return a face
without sensing its accomplishment, water
so different in the final armslength
of daylight, seeming to soften as it darkens
but really only darkening after all, and even then
my mirror bent over the evening water,
the voice of objects saying *love what*
refuses you and the voice of heaven saying
praise your correspondence with all things
beautiful there below, and my own voice
assigned to ask *O behold my heart.*

Inseminator Man

When I call him back now, he comes dressed in the silver of
    memory,
silver coveralls and silver boots
and a silver hard hat that makes no sense.
The cows could not bombard his head,
though the Lilies and Buttercups, the Jezebels and Mathildas,
avenged their lot in other ways
like kicking over a pail or stomping his foot.
Blue welt, the small bones come unknitted,
the big toenail a black cicada peeling off its branch.

———————

It wasn't hard to understand their grudge, their harbor
    of accumulated hurts —
imagine lugging those big tits everywhere, year after year.
Balloons full of wet concrete
hung between their legs like scrotums, duplicate and puffed.
I remember grappling with the nipples
like a teenage boy in a car's back seat
and how the teats would always fill again before I could complete
    their squeezing-out.
At night, two floors above them in the half-demolished barn,
my hands ached and made me dream of cows that drained
until the little stool rose off the ground and I found myself
    dog-paddling in milk.

———————

The summer after college I'd gone off to live with women
who'd forsworn straight jobs and underwear and men.
At night the ten of us linked hands
around a low wirespool table before we took our meals of
    vegetables and bread.
Afterward, from where the barn's missing wall
opened out on Mad River, which had no banks but cut an oxbow
flush with the iridescent green swale of the lower fields,
I saw women bathing, their white flanks in dim light
rising like mayflies born straight out of the river.

———————

Everyone else was haying the lower field when he pulled up,
his van unmarked and streamlined like his wares:
vials of silvery jism from a bull named Festus
who — because he'd sired a jersey that took first place
at the Vermont state fair in '53 —
was consigned to hurried couplings with an old maple stump
rigged up with white fur and a beaker.
When the man appeared I was mucking stalls in such heat
that I can't imagine whether or not I would have worn
    my shirt
or at what point it became clear to me that the bull Festus had been dead for
    years.

———————

I had this idea the world did not need men:
not that we would have to kill them personally
but through our sustained negligence they would soon die off
like houseplants. When I pictured the afterlife
it was like an illustration in one of those Jehovah's Witness
    magazines,
all of us, cows and women, marching on a promised land
colored that luminous green and disencumbered by breasts.
I slept in the barn on a pallet of fir limbs,
ate things I dug out of the woods,

planned to make love only with women, then changed my mind
when I realized how much they scared me.

———————

"Inseminator man," he announced himself, extending a hand,
though I can't remember we actually spoke.
We needed him to make the cows dry off and come into new milk:
we'd sell the boy-calves for veal, keep the females for milkers,
and Festus would live on, with this man for a handmaid,
whom I met as he was either going into the barn or coming out.
I know for a fact he didn't trumpet his presence,
    but came and went mysteriously
like the dove that bore the sperm of God to earth.

———————

He wore a hard hat, introduced himself before I took him in,
and I remember how he graciously ignored my breasts while still
    giving them wide berth.
Maybe I wore a shirt or maybe not: to say anything
    about those days now sounds so strange.
We would kill off the boys, save the females for milkers
    I figured,
as I led him to the halfway mucked-out stalls, where he
    unfurled a glove past his elbow
like Ava Gardner in an old-movie nightclub scene.
Then greased the glove with something from a rusted can
    before I left him in the privacy of barn light
with the rows of cows and the work of their next generation
while I went back outside to the shimmering and nearly
    blinding work of mine.

Lost Innocence of the Potato Givers

They're just a passing phase. All are symptoms of our times and the confusion around us.
— Reverend Billy Graham on The Beatles

At first we culled our winnings from the offering
    of fists —
one potato, two potato — until we realized that such
    random calibration
was no real test of love. So we cultivated pain:
hunkering on the macadam
sun-baked for hours in the schoolyard, our panties
    bunched beneath our skirts.
The girl who could sit there longest would gain title
    to the most handsome Beatle, Paul.
John George Ringo — the rest were divvied according to
    whose buttocks were most scarlet.
And when our fourth-grade teacher asked why we wore such
    tortured looks through long division,
we shrugged, scritching our pencils over fleshy shapes
    of hearts and flowers.

Ed Sullivan started it, his chiseled and skeletal stub
    of a head, his big shoe
stomping our loyalties to the man-boys Dion
    and Presley.
Even priggish neighbor Emily said I had to kneel before
    the TV as though praying.
Then the pixels assembled the audience's exploding
    like a carcass when it's knifed,
and I copied the pose assumed on-screen: hands pressed
    against sides of my skull
like the bald dwarf who stands goggle-eyed on a jetty
    in Munch's painting, and screams.
My mother rushed to the basement, a dishrag dripping
    from her soaped hand.

What's wrong? she yelled. *Are you hurt? What in godsname*
    is all this screaming?

February 1964: Johnson's choppers were whopping up the sky
    over the Gulf of Tonkin.
Despite the tacit code of silence about the war, somehow
    they must have known:
on television, girls were brawling drunkenly and raking
    fingernails across their cheeks,
ripping their own hair in vicious chunks, as though beauty
    were suddenly indulgent or profane.
That night in Saigon's Capital Kinh-Do Theatre, three GIs
    got blown up during a strip show.
But of course I didn't know that. I couldn't have even
    found Saigon on a map.
Girls were going limp in the arms of riot-geared policemen,
    who carried them off like the dead,
and my mother was stunned when she saw I'd torn my shirt
    over my not-yet-breasts.

After that, I kept everything a secret, the self-inflicted
    burns and scars and nicks.
I was doing it for love love love: the stones in my shoes,
    the burrs in my shirt,
the mother-of-pearl penknife I used for cutting grooves
    in my thumb or palm
whenever I needed to swear some blood pact with another
    disenthralled potato giver.
We spent recess practicing how to stick our tongues
    in Paul's imaginary mouth,
letting everything drain out until we were limp, nothing,
    sucked right into the earth.
Then we would mash our bodies against the schoolyard's wide
    and gray-barked beech,
which was cruel and strong and unrelenting, smooth and cold,
    the way we hoped our husbands would be.

From the Devotions

I.
As if somewhere, away, a door had slammed shut.
— But not metal; not wood.

Or as when something is later remembered only
as something dark in the dream:

torn, bruised, dream-slow
descending, it could be anything —

tiling, clouds,
you again, beautifully consistent, in no

usual or masterable way   *leaves, a woman's*
shaken-loose throat, shattered

eyes of the seer, palms, ashes, the flesh
instructing; you, silent.

A sky, a sea requires crossing and, like that,
there is a boat or, like that, a plane:

for whom is it this way now, when
as if still did I lie down beside, still

turn to, touch
                    I can't, I could not save you?

II.
Not, despite what you believed, that
all travel necessarily ends here, at the sea.

I am back, but only because.
As the sun only happens to meet the water

in such a way that the water becomes
a kind of cuirass: how each piece takes

and, for nothing, gives back whatever light —
sun's, moon's. A bird that is not a gull

passes over; I mark what you would: underneath,
at the tip of either wing, a fluorescent-white

moon, or round star. Does the bird itself
ever see this? According to you   *many have*

had the ashes of lovers strewn here,
on this beach   on this water that now beats at,

now seems to want just to rest alongside.
The dead can't know we miss them   Presumably,

we were walking   *that we are walking*
upon them.

III.
All night, again,
a wind that failed to bring storm —

instead, the Paradise dream: the abandoned
one nest at a bad angle — in danger,

and what it is to not know it;
the equally abandoned one tree that,

. . .

for the time being, holds it — alone,
and what it is to not know it.

All morning, it has been the fog
thinning at last,

as if that were the prayer,
the streets filling with men   *as if they*

were divine answer and not just
what happens.   Do I love less, if less is

all I remember? Your mouth, like a hole
to fly through. What you understood

of the flesh: how always first are we
struck down.   *Then we rise; are astounded.*

The Kill

The last time I gave my body up,

to you, I was minded
briefly what it is made of,
what yours is, that

I'd forgotten, the flesh
which always
I hold in plenty no

little sorrow for because — oh, do
but think on its predicament,
and weep.

. . .

We cleave most entirely
to what most we fear
losing. We fear loss

because we understand
the fact of it, its largeness, its
utter indifference to whether

we do, or don't
ignore it. By then, you
were upon me, and then

in me, soon the tokens
I almost never can let go of, I'd
again begin to, and would not

miss them: the swan,
unfolding
upward less on trust than

because, simply, that's
what it does; and the leaves
leaving; a single arrow held

back in the merciless
patience which, in taking
aim, is everything; and last,

as from a grove in
flame toward any air
more clear, the stag, but

this time its bent
head a chandelier, rushing
for me, like some

• • •

undisavowable
distraction. I looked back,
and instead of you, saw

the soul-at-labor-to-break-its-bonds
that you'd become. I tensed
my bow:

one animal at attack,
the other — the other one
suffering, and love would

out all suffering —

Trade

Bending — as no
flower bends —
casting the difficult rule

of his attention upon an elsewhere
that accordingly broke open
into a splendor that, too,

would pass,
I am resigned,
mostly,

said the emperor,
to a history between us less of loss than,
more protractedly, of losing —

• • •

and, having said as much, said
nothing else to the man to
whom he'd said it;

whom, for years now, he'd called
variously paramour,
consort,

sir; who, for
himself, said nothing;
who from where he was seated could

see, and easily,
each at its labelled and color-coded slip
moored slackly,

the bows of the ships of the Fleet
Imperial, about which
what he found, just

then, most worth admiring it
is impossible, anymore, to
say exactly:

the trim of them,
flawless, sleek — reminiscent, in
that way, of almost any line from Ovid; or,

when there was wind,
how the bows tipped,
idly,

in it;
or the stillness, afterwards,
that they found; or the way they seemed to.

from *Plot*

Section 1

Submerged deeper than appetite

she bit into a freakish anatomy. the hard plastic of filiation.
a fetus dream. once severed. reattached. the baby femur
not fork-tender though flesh. the baby face now anchored.

What Liv would make would be called familial. not foreign.
forsaken. she knew this. tried to force the scene. focus the
world. in the dream. snapping the crisp rub of thumb to index.
she was in rehearsal with everyone. loving the feel of cartilage.
ponderous of damaged leaves. then only she. singing internally.
only she revealed. humming. undressing a lullaby: *bitterly,*
bitterly, sinkholes to underground streams . . .

In the dream waist-deep. retrieving a fossilized pattern forming
in attempt to prevent whispers. or poisoned regrets. reaching into
reams and reams. to needle seam a cord in the stream. as if
a wish borne out of rah rah's rude protrusion to follow the rest
was sporded. split. and now hard-pressed to enter the birth.

In the dream the reassembled desire to conceive wraps the
tearing placenta to a walled uterus. urge formed complicit. First
portraying then praying to a womb ill-fitting. she grows fat.

The drive in utero is fiction-filled. arbiter of the cut-out infant.
and mainstreamed. Why birth the other. to watch the seam rip.
to roughly conjoin the lacerating generations. lineage means to

step here on the likelihood of involution. then hard not to notice
the depth of rot at the fleshy roots.

To this outbreak of doubt. she crosses her legs. the weight of one
thigh on the next. constructed rectitude. the heavy. heavy.
devotion to no.

Ersatz

outside of this insular-traffic a woman in pink underlining the
alias gender. who is she really. call her. could you. would
you. call her. Mommy.

The hope under which Liv stood.

her craven face. it clamored. the trumpeter announced it.
she stood more steady then. marveling at her stammering.
hammering heart. collecting a so invisible breath. feeling
extreme. commencing. deeper than feeling was.

She wanted what he had been told she'd want. what she was.
expecting. then the expecting was also a remembering.
remembering to want. she was filling her mouth up with his —

yet it was not. it was not. the sound of sucking on the edge of
sleep. not soft brush of cheek. not the heat of the hand along
the neck.

There is a depiction. picture. someone else's boy gorgeously
scaled down. and crying out. and she not hearing. not having.
not bearing Ersatz —

She was filling her mouth up with his name. yet it was not.
it was not.

Liv forever approaching the boy like toddler to toy. the
mothering more forged than known. the coo-coo rising air

bubbles to meet colostrum. yellow. to blue. to milk. not having
to learn. knowing by herself. come closer —

in front the glare. pools in straining veins making Liv
nervy. malachite half moons on each lobe listening inward.
the hormonal trash heap howling back.

There is dust from a filed nail. the wind lifts. carries it into
available light: not monochromatic. not flattened though
isolating. solicitous. soliciting. come closer —

Once Liv thought pregnancy would purify. you Ersatz
lacing lots. her pace of guilt. her site of murmur.

Then of course. of course. when do we not coincide elsewhere
with the avoided path. a sharp turn toward the womb-shaped
void. now

Liv is feeling in vitro. duped. a dumbness of chimes. no
smiles for every child so careful. so careful.

Ersatz

infant. bloomed muscle of the uterine wall. you still pink
in the center. resembling the saliva slick pit of the olive.
resembling tight petals of rose. assembling

Ersatz

This. his name was said. Afterward its expression wearing
the ornate of torment. untouched by discretion. natural light
or (so rumored

(and it. once roused. caused ill-ease as if kissed full on the
mouth.

. . .

Herself assaulting the changing conditions, Liv added
desire's stranglehold. envisaged its peculiarly pitched ache
otherwise alien to her wildly incredulous hopes: Ersatz

Ersatz

aware of your welt-rising strokes. your accretion of theme. Liv
was stirring (no. breathing the dream. she was preventing a trust
from forming. still the bony attachment was gaining its tissue
like a wattle and daub weave.

Ersatz

arrival is keyhole-shaped. it allows one in the assembled warren
of rooms. to open the game box even as the other leans against
the exposed from her freestanding. exaggerated perspective.

She is on her way in the corridor unable to enter this room
and if she prays to be released from you. as one would
pray to be released from tinnitus or welt. boy ridge of flesh
raised by a blow.

imagine in your uncurl of spinal arch. her eye your eye. an
apparition hushed to distortion. her heart unclosed. yet warped
by dullness and pure feeling. her lips but a crease recrossing
time. needing a softer tone.

Imagine the prayer itself

Ersatz

unswallowed. swollen within her lips. so grieved:

Ersatz,

here. Here. I am here

. . .

inadequately and feeling more and more less so because of not feeling more, but stopped. For I am of course frightened of you, what your bold face will show me of me. I am again leading to regret. I have lived, Ersatz, the confusion in my head, the fusion that keeps confusion. Could it keep you? Could it make those promises to remedy tortuous lines, thickening encroachings?

Oh, Ersatz, my own, birth is the limiting of the soul, what is trapped with it already owns. I could quadruple my intent toward you, be your first protection; but I could not wish a self on any self as yet unformed, though named and craved.

Ersatz,

I am here. And here is not analogous to hope.

See past the birth into these eyes of yours, into what increasingly overstates resemblance, a semblance one might wish to tuck under, into the sweat of the armpit, into its wiry odor of exhaustion, remembering the self and any reflection thereof is never a thing to cradle.

Ersatz,

were I coward enough to have you, child, coward enough to take my pain and form it into a pulsing, coming round the corner any odd day, of course, of course, I would believe you the intruder, had intruded.

Provoked, Ersatz, the best I could be would be shivering illness, mucus rising, the loud rush, the sob.

I am made uncomfortable and more so, no warmer, no closer to the everyone you are. Already the orphan, suffocating and overlapping a trillion faces —

• • •

are you utterly anywhere. have we, have we arrived anywhere.

Ersatz,

has the rudimentary ear curled open. are you here?

Cerberus

Failure isn't a swamp of quicksand or a mist,
It's just a mirror. The intractable is clear,
Though strangely unfamiliar, yellowing buildings,
New white and silver ones, the dirt lane
That slowly disappears through swaying
And indifferent grass. The crack
At the heart of your character decent people
Couldn't find with a spotlight
Or a blinking neon sign crying soundlessly
Inside its red arrow: *"Here! Here!"*
Is instantly apparent to any criminal
Or cunning muscle-man, so relaxed
They're as good as affable: "Old friend,"

They'll whisper with a wet grin, "what a struggle
You've had! But that's over. I'm wholly in charge
And couldn't care less where you've been!"
But still you'll continue to mumble,
Lying through your teeth, as if the pale,
Powerful, sympathetic freak
Wearing the flared wig and mask
Of intuitive insensitivity were actually
Your life's companion: "I've attained
So much success, I don't know where to begin!"
But nothing's as bored with history as the end.
The mind's three brains were made for diversion,
And everyone wags roughly the same tale.

The Sofia Buslot

The busses, like fruit-peddlers' horses,
Were adorned with plastic vines and flowers:
Morning glories, or else in the mind of wait-and-hurry
Violets grew on strands of ivy. Gas was costly.
Busses departed by secret plan. Meanwhile
Three filthy women stood grilling and selling
Sausage sandwiches, a fat blonde,
A nervous brunette, and an impervious
Black-haired Bulgarian — Bulgar being a city
In western Mongolia, the buslot
A bazaar transplanted from Asia,
Didn't have to go far.

Two dogs watched business,
An optimistic puppy, and a mother
With drooping tits, thus also an optimist,
Though with the wisdom of misery.
They hoped for snacks, for sausage mishaps.
Bad things happen. A bitch's misfortunes
Are a bastard's delight, and vice versa.
As for the *fatale* female trio, the sisters
Twisting and dispensing sausages
Over gas fires, they were immune
To sentimental charm: the puppydog
Got kicked, but the bitch
Knew when to duck and quit.

After watching the brunette
Adjust her ponytail, test the bounce
Of her bangs, and entertain a few stout men
By rubbing lard on a sausage in white
Intestinal skin, I purchased a navel orange
From a resentful witch, and back
On my throbbing, paralyzed bus,
Ill-advisedly swallowed its plump,
Unprotected belly-button.

That's what made me sick when I got home
From Istanbul, where the only belly-dancers I saw
Were on postcards. In the Sofia buslot,
I made the mistake of thinking
I could escape fate.

Bulgarian Girl

Live with a fox at your heart and deny it proudly,
Constantly, calmly, like that Bulgarian girl
Who'd stolen a vixen she knew would maraud
Her family's chickens: infuriating, its tail
Stirring as it chewed through her sternum
Plunging its teeth into her heart's right atrium,
Rearing its red-black bush beneath the blouse
Her interrogators tore from her suddenly
One-breasted body as she swooned, perished,
The fox, her gore dripping from its muzzle,
Wide-eyed as a baby. Her cousins, or descendants,
Live near mountains from which the Romans,
When they came, extracted ore, but her mother
Gave her those eyes which shone with water
Richer than glass, the hair of crows who'd mingled
Long ago with doves, a breast so lovely and small
It couldn't interfere with access to her heart.

Striking a Match

Notes scratched for an introduction
I made ten years ago for a friend's lecture:
"*Voices wrapped in the gift each sex possesses
Of not listening to the other,*" and how,
"*Desire is always an impulse toward archaic forms.*"
I instantly suffered a leap of envious regret,

My sentences mingled with his so distant
And intelligent: that metaphor of voices as wrappings
Which slip at the promise of a climax deferred,

And inattentiveness as a sexual disguise
Of mind reading the Braille of an impulse
Toward a more "archaic form." How I wanted
To share with someone this thought, always
The opposite of desire. Then sadness
Could explode like a stick match and burn
With a yellow fire, for if there's a form more archaic,
We don't pay much attention to it, and of course
About the innocence of thought, that's so wrong.

Redbird, Soon in the Morning

Gazing again at those crimson
Morning glory berries clustered
In the lilac branches, thinking
Mistakenly they were the cardinal,
Then remembering Leadbelly's
Reel for children, so simple, sweet,

Amused and teasing, a murderer's
Lullaby seasoned with yearning:
O Baby, the Not Yet is Now. Berries
So red and puffy they're poisonous,
And the green hearts of the lilac
Just jealous — "Soon in the morning . . ."

The Wine-Dark Sea

Black dandelions amid a few ordinary daisies.
    Very sexy, but you smell a rat: God,
    Reaching into a cloud and pulling out
A stallion of a sun sulphurous as a horse's plum
Pitching harmless knives at the spinning ocean.
The bumblebee is unconfused. It keeps mumbling

    Homerically, as I do, *"Oinopa ponton!*
Oinopa ponton!," and dives for the tunnel,
The honey and the money. The sea and pasture
Lie with their eyes closed, smiling as you do,
Not wanting to miss the subtlest soft surprise.
Or wiggle as a cloud passes, mermaid gauze,

And suddenly out of the water plunges Proteus
Spritzing a geyser. Old Faithful. Hot as a kiss.

Reminder

Torment by appetite
is itself an appetite
dulled by inarticulate,
dogged, daily

loving-others-to-death —
as Chekhov put it, "compassion
down to your fingertips" — ,
looking on them as into the sun

not in the least for their sake
but slowly for your own
because it causes
the blinded soul to bloom

like deliciousness in dirt,
like beauty from hurt,
their light — *their* light —
pulls so surely. Let it.

A Good Father

The cancer's eaten half his liver.
The bile's going to the brain.
With one night more at most to live,
he's acting insane.

. . .

The food his family brings is poison.
Not one of them has ever cared.
What a life he would have lived without them,
if only he'd dared.

Conversations while he's sleeping —
in the hallway, on the phone —
link his dear ones in forgiveness
while he alone

joins the torments of resentment
swelling to its highest power
that will take him like a whirlwind
across the river of fire.

A Two-Year-Old Girl in a Restaurant

Your delight, which is contagious,
has been occasioned by
the twinkling point of a steak knife
about to liquefy your eye,

so when your father swats it
from your prehensile fist
you squinch your blooming face
tight as a blastocyst

as if all the world's pain
had conceived inside your skull
and you, the prima diva
of the coloratura wail,

go deep into your soul
to sing how such pain feels,
and we remember well
and smile or do not smile.

Birthday

The years I've lost to selfishness
bivouacked at midnight on my lawn,
aimed an arsenal at the house,
trucked in their dates, and partied till dawn.

They all got plenty drunk enough
to blow the whole neighborhood to smoke,
but not one touched the lethal guns,
which apparently is the joke

they think they think of when they convene
at the local Motel Six,
where they commandeer the ice machine
and gorge on Cheddar Stix

before the Annual Benefit Brawl
to celebrate the teeth
with which they rip their faces off
and my face underneath.

Every Sunday

Psychotic homeless boy
blocking our exit from the church —
straggle-haired, bloated,
eyes shining like ice —

doing his rooster-pecking thing
with his hand made the beak
into each of our faces
as we file out —

or is it snake-striking
or airhole-punching

or just compulsive counting us
one and one and one?

He will not live long.
He will allow the pastor
to wrap an arm around his shoulder,
and lead him to coffee and crullers.

But to *be* him

Wings of the Morning

She says her heart is ripped
because of him, and he
might reply he tried to help her see
before their life together stopped

and then gave up: Just look
at all these *things* you bought!,
he was about to shout,
as if the deep-glazed vase she took

time and attention to find
and placed just so to show
dawn light through their window
could seem to shine for him

had been responsible for what
his life is not, or now her filmy
curtains suddenly beautifully
shaping the breeze they caught.

The Present Perfect

I saw the cells on TV, as they swam
up to the egg, tails lashing, and I heard
the wind-tunnel sound they make, the steady hum

of thousands, blind, threadlike, worn, but soaring
through waterfalls in their drive to live, move,
and set the egg revolving like a star.

For us, there was no miracle of birth.
No genes, no geniuses. And yet, OK,
we had other things: our work, our history

scrawled on Margaux labels and libretti,
and, after all, no cribs, no sticky plums,
no pulling paper napkins, one by one,

from a metal box, to mop up dumped ice cream.
But then again, no immortality:
in my religion, children to speak my name

after I am. No heir to your kindness,
your skill with a kite, your father's whimsey,
or to my mother's mother's diamond pin.

And yet, we had each other's silences;
freedom to wander with no fixed plan,
now fixed in photos of sylphs that resemble us,

. . .

peering down cliffs in Brittany at ragged boards
floated up from dinghies lost at sea,
searching for fish carved into chapels' altars,

spending our suns like out-of-date coins,
until we reached the present-perfect tense —
that have-been state where past and future merge:

We have been married thirty-four years.
I see the kids we were frisk on this lawn
in the late afternoon's unnameable light.

Too late for them, and for their unborn kids,
but not too late for us, here among cedars,
to praise the fires in rose petals on slate;

white rhododendrons, a fountain's rainbow.
I see the dot of you, meadows away,
that grows in sight as you pedal home;

your reddish hair and beard, now tarnished silver,
that once we wanted for a chromosome;
your silhouette in a Manet-like straw hat

as you bless your new astilbe: "Live and be well,"
casting aside your customary questions
for an irrational faith the plant will grow;

I hear your voice that calls me to see wildflowers
poking through gravel cracks in our neighbors' driveway,
slender but fortunate, built to last their day.

American Solitude

The cure for loneliness is solitude. — Marianne Moore

Hopper never painted this, but here
on a snaky path his vision lingers:

Three white tombs, robots with glassed-in faces
and meters for eyes, grim mouths, flat noses,

lean forward on a platform, like strangers
with identical frowns scanning a blur,

far off, that might be their train.
Gas tanks broken for decades face Parson's

smithy, planked shut now. Both relics must stay.
The pumps have roots in gas pools, and the smithy

stores memories of hammers forging scythes
to cut spartina grass for dry salt hay.

The tanks have the remove of local clammers
who sink buckets and stand, never in pairs,

but one and one and one, blank-eyed, alone,
more serene than lonely. Today a woman

rakes in the shallows, then bends to receive
last rays in shimmering water, her long shadow

knifing the bay. She slides into her truck
to watch the sky flame over sand flats, a hawk's

wind arabesque, an island risen, brown
Atlantis, at low tide; she probes the shoreline

. . .

and beyond grassy dunes for where the land
might slope off into night. Hers is no common

emptiness, but a vaster silence filled
with terns' cries, an abundant solitude.

Nearby, the three dry gas pumps, worn
survivors of clam-digging generations,

are luminous, and have an exile's grandeur
that says: In perfect solitude, there's fire.

One day I approached the vessels
and wanted to drive on, the road ablaze

with dogwood in full bloom, but the contraptions
outdazzled the road's white, even outshone

a bleached shirt flapping alone
on a laundry line, arms pointed down.

High noon. Three urns, ironic in their outcast
dignity — as though, like some pine chests,

they might be prized in disuse — cast rays,
spun leaf-covered numbers, clanked, then wheezed

and stopped again. Shadows cut the road
before I drove off into the dark woods.

Last Requests

are clear in books: "Dorset, embrace him . . .
And make me happy in your unity";
and in old movies: "Take care of my hyacinths."
In opera, last pleas fill the diva's arias.

I've waited for last hopes, my amulets
against silence. My father, dying, spoke
in an urgent Polish he'd not used in years,
but his words, staccato trumpet notes,

were not injunctions. When my mother's life
crested like a wave before it breaks,
I asked her wishes. She said, "Ice cream, quick!"
and hurled a glance that said she was not in pain

but dying, and must hurry on with it.
Lips trembled open: "Don't kiss me again.
No, you catch everything. But thanks for coming."
Then quiet. In a trance, a captive audience,

she could not clamp my vows, but not a syllable
I uttered had been left unsaid in tiffs,
snarls at ogres in the stories told
on rainy days until the china mugs

rattled on glass shelves, in alphabet games,
nouns binding us like ropes we strung with beads
and lifted up, verbs spinning like bedsheets
we dried, then pulled taut. Words were for wishing

on first daffodils, secrets kept from others.
Now I'll take any edict, fiat, murmur,
gossip, or prayer. Hers, not another's.
When the phone rang at dawn I thought, wrong number,

. . .

and blurred the verdict. Even expecting it,
I was not prepared, nor will I be
in her rooms, tapping a crystal bowl,
waiting for words to burn through it like sun.

Poem Ending with a Phrase from the Psalms

Here where loss spins the hickory's dry leaves,
rolls miles under wheels, and bleaches reeds
that shone wine-red, I invoke a rose
still rising like a choir, past its prime
on a spindly bush that bore scarce blooms,
as I wake to hear a jay screech like a gate
swung open, and see your hand enfolding mine
on linen: *teach us to number our days.*

Definition of the Soul

after Pasternak

The attempt to separate my soul from yours
is like wringing out a handkerchief
wet from something spilled.

I remember the burned-down house
where a wreath still hung on the door,
a wreath, stone-white, to our surprise,
useless, forlorn, like a life-preserver
nailed to the shore's churning rubble.

You said the flames went off somewhere,
strengthened, more vile than ever,
perhaps seeking a child's crib.

When speeding tires lofted street-water
onto your dress, I admired how you. . . .

And afterward, I brushed your hair,
as you lay dozing on the couch,
your lower lip, a perfect, promising V.

The attempt to separate my soul from yours
is like the creaking of a lamppost
against a sapling in the wind.
Soon someone will come
and hack through the more fragile one.

After Surgery

Walking the hall
was like circling the dance floor
the night Piggy's got strobe lights.
Just as you sidestepped the waitress
she clanged you with her tray,
the eclipse too quick
for those of us laboring
under the ruling constellations,
slaving like ice in tumblers of gin.
A codeine sleep our sole release
except for baseball,
a pleasure wrecked all week
by the ubiquitous presence
of a part-time catcher from Chicago
named Karkovice
whose name boiled up in fever dreams
as a refrain
that tugged my head
from one side of the bed to the other.
Karkovice, a voodoo doctor
mixing a potion called "Jazz Drool."
Karkovice, the tarpit that flummoxed
the last mastodon.
Karkovice, an overthrown dictator
manacled to his wife.
Karkovice, the phrase, in Stupka,
for "more than enough."
Karkovice, the thick lip
that drops off a highway
when the dirt road begins.

Mop String

Everything in my hospital room
remained photograph-still
during my two-week stay
except for the inch of string
pushed loose from the mop
by the maid's exuberant sloshing.
Pet-like, it hid in a new corner
each day, dragged to the door
by the surgeon's four-pound brogan,
or plastered to the molding,
a convict pinned against
the perimeter wall
to evade the searchlight,
parched, doused, stiffened again
with a pine scent.
Just before they wheeled me
through the exit's glass doors,
I picked it up.
Sunlight leapt upon the windows
of the airport bus,
onto rows of bandaged passengers
pressing their incisions
at each sharp turn,
and the pungent inch,
the rough charm
that kept me company
while my drilled skull throbbed,
seemed lost, not saved,
as it unfurled along the lifeline
of my palm.

History

If we stare too far ahead
we trip over the feeblest root.

If we look back
we become shadows,
people who pick up accents
from a long stay in a strong country.

If we take too much care,
fearful of the god
whose footfalls we hear approaching,
we go nowhere,

caught in the song
of our age,
the flickering storm of ash
from the raked leaves,

and in the flurry,
a black butterfly
batting the air
as it dips through the cinders.

Which one's on fire?
Which has a home in this world?

Front Street

Neither of us had an easy winter
though it must have looked like it,
sitting at a window on the bay
with glasses of whiskey.
The low tide brought birdlife, dogs,
bits of clay or porcelain plate,

and tourists taking the lazy way to town.
High tide covered everything
right up to the porch, and one day
we lost our tempers over it.
Arguing with the powers of the moon
is a losing business, and by spring
he went off to a high-paying job,
A.A. meetings and no time
even to breathe the spring air.
I left to teach in a floral suburb
with the same detriments.
The tides don't miss us,
nor the landlord who owned
that waterfront property,
nor Gerald the cat
who we squirted with pistols
when he crept up on the tern nests.
And Susan and Shelley, where are they?
The sea and its tides
must be having a laugh
on the two guys who fell
for their heroic example,
fatal to mortals,
of starting over and over again.

The Burned Boy

The burned boy rode the tilt-a-whirl
at our small town fair,
and as his half-shell
shot through the noon sky
I watched his eyes
divide from his head
when he turned the sharp circle
that sped everyone to the false death
promised by the ride.

From the railing where I stood,
all grins raged
into a pulled-back, wind-torn parade,
as if each face
snagged on a thorn and kept going
through the churchyard lot
which drowsed with the chords
of a staticky organ,
booths of fundamentalists and biscuits,
and nothing to do
with our children
in the afternoon
but watch them strain
in their locked seats
against vaulting into the airy gauze
known here as the heavens,
and believed to answer every prayer.

Augusto Jandolo: On Excavating an Etruscan Tomb

"When we lit our torches
My eyes went blind in the cave's
Cool dark —
                the damp rock rough against my palms,
I remember how we strained to lift
                        the great stone lid: slowly
It rose, stood on end . . . then fell
Heavily aside, crashing down
                  in the smoky,
Turbulent light
So that just for an instant I saw —
It wasn't a skeleton I saw;
                not bones,
But a body, the arms and legs stiffly outstretched —
A young warrior's flesh still dressed
In armor, with his helmet, spear, shield, and greaves
As though he'd just been laid in the grave:

For just that moment
Inside the sarcophagus I saw the dead live —
                      but then, beneath
The sea-change of our torches,
At the first touch of air, the warrior
Who'd lain there, his body inviolable
For centuries, dissolved —
                dissolved, as we looked on,
Into dust . . .
          his helmet rolling right, his round shield sagging
Into the void beneath his breastplate, the greaves
Collapsing as his thighs gave way . . .

. . .

                              But in the aura
Round our torches a golden powder
Rose up in the glow and seemed to hover."

Newsreel

It was like being in the crosshairs of a magnifying glass
Or the beams of the planets concentrating in a death ray
Passing right through me, boring a hole between

My shoes through the concrete floor all the way
To the far side of the earth. Yet it was only
Not knowing how to get where I was going,

I'd gotten lost in the parking lot on the way
To the cinder block bunker where my mother
Worked the snackbar, my father the projector.

The drive-in movie screen stretched horizon
To horizon, the whole of Texas sprawled around,
Cathedral-like De Sotos and great-finned Pontiacs

Flickering and sinister in torrents of light flooding
Down the screen. Frozen in that light, I
Might have been the disconsolate ageless

Stone-eyed child ornamenting a pillar
In a dead Roman city high up on a desert plateau.
I wasn't even as tall as the speakers mumbling

On and on the way now in my dream of extreme
Old age I hear voices mumbling interminably . . .
Where does it shimmer, my refuge, grotto of my swimming pool

•   •   •

Lapping in the infinite leisure of the newsreel?
At last my mother appeared from among the cars
And led me back to the snackbar but I still hovered

Out there, turned loose among the shadows'
Disembodied passions striving for mastery
Above the tensed windshields: There gleams

Marilyn Monroe movie star enjoying her fame
In the voluptuous, eternal, present tense
Of celebrity being worked over by hands

Of her masseur. Bougainvillea overgrows
Her beach bungalow retreat of peace and pleasure,
The screen nothing now but layer on layer

Of flesh the fingers knead in a delirious ballet
Pushing, pulling, palms slippery and quick,
Ambiguous instruments of comfort or of pain.

The rush of blood to her face clouds into
White light as film stock jerks across
A void half coma blackout, half nightmare aura:

The film jammed, raw light pulsing like a bandage
On a face wrapped round and round in surgical gauze.
Wherever that light took me looms far from candy bars

And gum wrappers blazing under glass. The movie poster
Death ray stopped the earth revolving, time had stopped,
My mother's black slacks and my father's not yet grown goatee,

My own hands shaking nervously about were silently dissolving
In that ray bombarding from beyond the galaxy
Being invaded by screeching, beseeching noises

•   •   •

Of alien beings searching for a planetary home.
Then, up there, on the screen, frenetic in the light,
Was a hair trembling between two cloven lobes

Of shadow that were part of the projector's
Overheating brain, its brilliantly babbling, delusional,
Possessed by shadows, dispossessed brain.

Prayer

after Horace

God of flesh, god of pleasure,
give us leisure while we're still strong —
                                                                    defend us
from the whirlwind that blights
ash leaves with lesions,
                                        that makes the black cypress shake
like the junkie I saw begging on the corner.

Calm the undertow of the sea,
make the world
                        go slow as shadows
shifting as the sun shifts
in the garden of Persephone.

We kneel at the foot of oblivion's alp,
waiting for the snow to melt,
                                        for the stream
fretted with ice
to crack like a pistol shot,
                                shatter
and flow
as we splash out wine staining the tablecloth.

• • •

Keep hidden from us what tomorrow holds —

let's go looking while we can, while the Zone
or the Block or Wareham Street
lures us down onto our knees at night,
                              through parks
and dunes, the Gladiator's Gym
and the Brass Rail . . .

Oh god of flesh, god of pleasure,

keep us in the dark
                    one moment more —

touching hands, lips grazing
lips, flesh
moving into flesh

 . . . as the sun goes down
to orgy in the snow
                    on Soracte's slopes
shadowy as bodies giving
                    themselves away.

The Dreamhouse

Does it move inside him, that trembling of the earth?
Or is it his spirit failing him, teetering and wobbling,
Its gyroscopic spin slowing to a swoon?

And when he mumbles of seven falls descending one into the next,
Is he the one stumbling up the spray-slick wooden steps,
Or is he himself the slowly diffusing spray?

• • •

That permeable ocean between him and his death
Overflows the window and lifts him above the waves,
His drenched sheets and his hands limp in his lap

Poised eternally, a bubble about to break . . .
And then the air thickens, weighing down his flesh,
The earth's trembling now too ghostly for him to feel,

The seven falls mere water pouring pool to pool,
His still body afloat in the ether of morphine
Expunged by the glare flooding across the pane . . .

His being, like absence new-minted in the clouds,
Scatters in gusts and squalls. Sheets stripped, his vacant bed
Hovers in the room while moonlight, sunlight

Scrub the walls clean — his closets now emptied,
His clothes dispersed, his face, his eyes doing
A slow dissolve in memory's salt baths

Even as he takes up residence, the dreamhouse
A void all glass and air: one table, one chair,
And sweeping wall to wall to wall sunlight everywhere.

Red Dog

We bought you for our son. Half-grown,
already your bag of skin sagged everywhere,
you fell to sleep like the dark in corners,
predictably where we wouldn't look under
wash piled and waiting, in closets, the moan
and wheeze of your easy breathing pointed
with pips and starts of other sounds, cries
rising, a chain of woof-woof-woofs soon to
decline like cars down the hill's far glide
of night where we said he might never go.
Of course he went, as with him went also you.

You dragged, then lost a bright steel chain: two tags
hung like my dad's world war loudly declared
"Red Dog," your name, our place, and that year's
shots, identities you'd shake off to wander
the possible world. I'd hear you, coming back,
my son still out looking, afraid you'd got
worse than traveler's bite on your mopy flanks.
His shoes puffed up dirt like spurts of time. You
mostly don't expect to find the lost — and yet,
hopeful, I'd shout, then sleep, then shout. Gone.
You'd wait. You'd creep like sun across the lawn,

then, with him, leap up everywhere, that Spring
of joy breaking roses, crushing mulched shoots
faithfully planted year after year, and roots
whose volunteers you watered dead. Soon we saw
he'd leave, you'd chase God knows what twitch
of spoor, and so we took your balls. You slowed.

Dirt-bedded, you had new smell. Bones fouled floors.
Squirrels reclaimed their nuts. The awful spew
of what spoiled in you, lying by our fire,
comes back to me as the vet says you've worn
out the heart that banged to sleep beside my son.

What does it sound like, I ask. The vet listens.
Once you climbed a six-foot fence, barking, one leap,
a storm of breath we loved. Now you only eat,
120 wheezing pounds, a processor of meat.
Like my dad, you face me, hesitate, then piss
blankets and floor. Deaf, eyes blank, the chain
slipped again, you're lost. You don't miss a boy's
games, nothing swells your interest, even the moon's
rattling tags I've hung above the waiting spades.
The vet claims it's time. We've let you go too far.
Calling at last, I say "Son. It's Red. Come home."

For Jeddie Smith

Of Oystermen, Workboats

The wide, white, wing-boned washboards of twenty
footers, sloped, ridged to hold
a man's tongs and stride,

                       the good stance
to scrape deep with a motion like big applause,
plunging the teeth true beyond the known
mounds of the dead, the current carried
cloisters of murk,
                miracles that bloom
luminous and unseen, sweet things to be
brought up, bejeweled, culled from husks,

. . .

as oystermen like odd angels glide far off enough
to keep a wake gentle as shirts on a line,
red baseball caps dipping like bloodied
heads upright, the clawed hands slapped
at the air in salute,
                    those washboards that splinter
the sun on tongs downlaid, on tines humming,

those womb-hulls harbored flank to flank at dusk
until the white-robed priest of the moon
stands tall to the sea's spume-pour
in nostrils
              of the men who sway from heel to heel,

the season come again, the socketed gray
of their eyes rolling outward,
forearms naked past longjohns,
the salted breast-beaters at first light

lined up, ready to fly.

Night Pleasures

Poquoson, Virginia

Where I come from land lies flat as paper.
      Pine, spruce, holly like dark words
left from a woods. Creeks coil, curve,
      enigmatic as women. To know the depths
you must dream. In the mountains
      for college I walked up and could see
barns, cows, housesmoke, but no boats.
      Hillsides of apples, still, perfect.

Here my little boat takes the night Bay.
      One far neon light tosses, a city

people walk alone, its rhythmic
        landscape cut from marshes and cries.
On black water it is all mine, first
        beginnings, endings, love's beauties.
So when I move, it moves under me, and knows me.

Making a Statement

Thousands, lately, have asked me about my hair.
Why is it so long? Why haven't you cut it?
I think about Samson, of course, and his woe.
His hair like thickets where I was born, swamps,
tall grasses bending with red-winged blackbirds
like a woman's nipples in the quick sun-gold.
I could tell about Samson, about the girl,
but I say my head is cold. I need cover.
Playing tennis with a leggy blonde I love,
I admit I can't do anything with it, my youth.
She rolls her eyes into a smashing serve.
"You old guys," she teases with her hot drop-shot.
Back and forth all day, yellow balls, long gray hair.

Descending

Remember that tin-foil day at the beach descending
on water the color of slate, the man descending,
just a bald head like an emptied melon descending
God knows where, same day a shy girl-child descending
with doll and bike to darkness where, descending
the hill with dumptruck vizor down, sun descending,
a father squints just once and the years descending
ever now spin him like a pump's flush-pipe descending
to pure waters he can never reach and, descending,
what of wings flamed gold, dusk's holy glow descending,

heron, tattered, wearied, news-heavy head descending,
that's left by hunters to float all night, descending
as they do into sleep, the earth clean, just descending?
Where, and with whom, are those we've seen descending?

At the Vet's

The German shepherd can't lift his hindquarters
off the tiled floor. His middle-aged owner
heaves his dog over his shoulder, and soon
two sad voices drift from the exam room
discussing heart failure, kidneys, and old age
while a rushing woman pants into the office
grasping a terrier with trembling legs
she found abandoned in a drainage ditch.
It's been abused, she says, and sits down,
the terrier curled in her lap, quaking
as the memory of something bad returns and returns.
She strokes its ears, whispering endearments
while my two cats, here for routine checkups,
peer through the mesh of their old green carrier,
the smell of fear so strong on their damp fur
I taste it as I breathe. Soon the woman,
like the receptionist with her pen in mid-air,
is listening, too, hushed by the duet
swelling in volume now, the vet's soprano
counterpointed by the owner's baritone
as he pleads with her to give him hope, the vet
trying to be kind, rephrasing the truth
over and over until it becomes a lie
they both pretend to accept. The act's over.
His dog's to stay behind for ultrasound
and kidney tests, and the man, his face
whipped by grief as if he were caught in a wind,
hurries past us and out the front door,
leaving the audience — cats, terrier, people —
sunk in their places, too stunned to applaud.

Dead Moth in a Bottle of Mineral Water

Before you pour me down the kitchen sink
or else return my bottle to the store,
let me explain. It's true I ruined your drink
but not on purpose. You see I meant to soar
on new lavender wings when I hatched out
from sticky larvae. I dreamed of wild nights
fluttering over the trees, floating about
the wide world so I could see great sights.
At last my body changed. Now for the fun.
I rustled my antennae, enraptured by
a bright glow I thought was the glorious sun
and flew straight up, not knowing I would die
fried by a light bulb moments after birth
inside a bottling plant, my sparkling earth.

Tatyana

She leaves the room. Onegin writhes
On stage, ashamed of his emotion.
He scorned her as a young girl.
Now he's mad about her! But she's
Married, rich, so stern and cold . . .
I lean forward in my opera seat.
There goes me. And isn't that
Every man I loved in vain?
The cast bows to wild applause.
Our Tatyana smiles, steps forward
To catch a bouquet of red roses.
I button my coat, grab my purse,
And make my slow way down the aisle
Of well-dressed, gray-haired couples
Watching their steps with downcast eyes.
I bet I'm not alone in wishing
I could go back in time, and break

A few cold hearts that broke mine
With all my hard-won understanding
Of the game of love, its rules
And stratagems, and power plays.
Then through the open lobby doors
Where the crowd hesitates, tying
Scarves or pulling on wool gloves,
I see the promised snow's begun
And someone's whistling an aria
From the first act. A sweet joy
Rushes through me. No, of course
I'd fall in love the same way.
I'd make every great mistake
I could, and earn this lovely moment
Walking home through fresh snow
My head full of unsingable music,
Remembering this one and that one
Who made me feel by feeling nothing.

Encounter on an Italian Beach

Is the storm over? The frothy sky's all cream.
Young men are sweeping the sand, setting up chairs.
I join early risers strolling the tide line,
And pass the last tourist hotel by the cliffs.
Now the beach is empty except for sandpipers,
Shell heaps, driftwood, and long strands of seaweed
Shining through descending gloom. The shush
Of heavy surf, mixed with the cries of sea gulls,
Sounds like an organ. Then I'm sure I do
Hear music, maybe a fisherman's radio.
But soon a crowd looms through the swirls of fog,
A blur at first, then resolving into the shapes
Of saints come down from Heaven to announce
The Last Judgment, and for a bad moment
My heart pounds, for there's no one here but me

On this chilly beach. Then I see they're humans
Led by a standard-bearer, his great flag rippling
As he leads his eerie crew along the shore,
Monks striding forward in swirling brown robes
Shoulder to shoulder with black cassocked priests,
And behind them ranks of scouts, tall girls and boys
In shorts and hiking boots. A burly fellow
Brings up the rear, hoisting a wooden cross
From which hang two speakers blaring out music,
The tune to the hymn that everyone's belting out.
No one glances my way. I might be a sea bird
Or simply someone beyond their apprehension —
Like a movie-goer watching them on film
Who sits on the edge of the soft, velvet seat
Disturbed by the surreal figures on the screen
That make no sense, but must mean something scary.
And yes, I've broken out in a cold sweat.
I run ahead until I spot café lights
Near where the railroad sweeps back again
To shore. As I reach the canvas awning,
Gusts of rain blow down from the racing clouds,
And I fling myself in a plastic chair to wait
For the real world to return with the sun —
Strewn over the golden sand like showy lilies,
Thousands of bright umbrellas, happy pagans.

Lost Life

His arm lightly clasps her shoulders
In this old black and white print
Of silver shades, and shadow tones
Created by exotic trees —
Palms, bananas, ferny acacia.
This is a garden in Paraguay,
And it's years and years ago.
They've dared the passage to the rim

Of Iguassu Falls in a small boat,
And survived that sharp fresh moment
When the mist merged with the roar.
I stare at them. Can they feel me
Musing over them like a giant
In this future where they've become
Icons of my own past?
What a romantic portrait this is,
Framed by an old friend who kept
The negative for twenty years.
Her long hair coils in tendrils
Over her brow, crammed with images
For the novel she's revising,
And his thick mustache catches gleams
As he broods on the brilliant poems
He'll publish later to applause.
Soon they'll rise and walk on,
Blasting each other with talk of art
And life's brevity. She won't hear
My awful sigh, like God's breath,
Just above this special non-
Reflecting glass. I grab a hammer.
Where shall I hang my younger self,
Upstairs, or down in the basement?
I remember debates about the age
Of the saved in heaven. Some said
We'd all be thirty-three like Christ
Crucified, but others claim
We'd be the age when we were purest.
I'll settle for this as paradise,
His arm around me, both of us
Glowing with passionate ignorance.

A Night in Assisi

I rubbed my eyes. How strange I felt. It was
As if a fissure in my brain had opened
Spilling out dreams. I sat in a small café
On the Piazza del Commune, where laughing kids
Practiced skits for a religious pageant
Dressed like angels, saints, Mary, even Christ
Grinning through a false beard as he showed off,
And the Wolf of Gubbio prancing upright —
The same crew I'd seen in the famous frescos
Of the Basilica. At ten o'clock bells
Rang out. Shouting, laughing, bursting into hymns,
The kids formed into lines and marched off.
Now murmuring voices lulled me as I sipped.
Tourists gabbled over drinks at other tables
Comparing Italian truffles to French,
Giotto to Cimabue, Assisi to Urbino . . .
I was so sleepy I seemed to understand
Words in languages I didn't speak
So I got up, yawning, and wandered uphill
Thinking the view might please me. And it did.
Mist floated like flimsy curtains on a stage
Down in the valley, while up above the moon
Illuminated the medieval churches,
Belltowers, refectories, and carved facades.
I leaned on a parapet, remembering
How I'd played a friar in a parish play
About St. Francis preaching to the birds.
My mother cut out a pattern, and stitched
Brown cloth on her old Singer in that life
Of faith and miracles I'd led as a child.
I'd write J.M.J. on the top of my tests,
And each night kneel to pray beside my bed.
How solid religion seemed, like the great town
Lined with stone buildings a thousand years old
That I'd walked through on the way up, never
Suspecting that below me plates of rock

Scraped forward on a molten sea, heading
For a collision that would crack churches,
Turn plaster saints to rubble and paint chips,
And topple towers where bright bells had pealed.

The Seasons

Ice-jammed hard-clasped branches in the blocks a whole river of them
        yet at the same time, the time sensed
beneath the time walked, the time breathing in and out, the water almost
        eddying, still pushing there beneath
the milk-white surface, deep down and over the bed of rocks; you could call
        them frozen, though they never live
another state than less and less until they're gone, the water going on and on
        until it all accrues again. The seasons
always seemed to be a form of freedom, something good for making meaning,
        the kind of notion a founding father could
pull out now and then whenever
        the now and then would flag. Time
healing time, you know the saw.
        Lightning strikes and struck.
The shepherd fell down dead.
And then it all wound up again: a red-breast made a ruckus, the quick eternal
  sprung.

You wanted summer or you wanted death.
        So death came, and that was autumn.

Two Brief Views of Hell

Leaving the fringe of light at the edge of the leaves, deep then deeper,
the rocking back and forth movement forward through the ever-narrowing
  circle
that never, in truth, narrowed beyond the bending going in,

not knowing whether a turn or an impasse would lie at the place
where the darkness turned into impenetrability, deep where
no longer could up or down or side to side be known, just the effort
to stay above the water, to keep one spread palm bearing up
against the weight and then the other, deeper and deeper.
The way in was easy once it began. The way in was all necessity.
Behind the darkness, more darkness; beneath the water only water.

A great black frayed trash bag lifted by the wind high above the sidewalk,
then just above the roofs, a black shining sail tattered, too big to be flying
and yet, each time it began its descent, lifted, propped up
and stiffened again in a sequence of small swirling movements.
The most oppressive thing,
the most tormenting, a black sun deflated, teasing,
touching the cornices and windows, block after block,
a hovering force, a curse, a smear.
The farther it rose in the distance, the larger it seemed to loom.
The mind wants an object and then recoils at what it has done.

The mind wants an object and then recoils at what it has done.
The farther it rose in the distance, the larger it seemed to loom.
a hovering force, a curse, a smear,
touching the cornices and windows, block after block,
the most tormenting, a black sun deflated, teasing,
the most oppressive thing
and stiffened again in a sequence of small swirling movements
and yet, each time it began its descent, lifted, propped up
then just above the roofs, a black shining sail tattered, too big to be flying
A great black frayed trash bag lifted by the wind high above the sidewalk.

Behind the darkness, more darkness; beneath the water only water.
The way in was easy once it began. The way in was all necessity.
against the weight and then the other, deeper and deeper.
to stay above the water, to keep one spread palm bearing up
no longer could up or down or side to side be known, just the effort
where the darkness turned into impenetrability, deep where
not knowing whether a turn or an impasse would lie at the place
that never, in truth, narrowed beyond the bending going in,

the rocking back and forth movement forward through the ever-narrowing
   circle
Leaving the fringe of light at the edge of the leaves, deep then deeper.

Let me tell you about my marvelous god

Let me tell you about my marvelous god, how he hides in the hexagons
of the bees, how the drought that wrings its leather hands
above the world is of his making, as well as the rain in the silent minutes
that leave only thoughts of rain.
An atom is working and working, an atom is working in deepest
night, then bursting like the farthest star; it is far smaller
than a pin-prick, far smaller than a zero and *it has no*
will, no will toward us.
This is why the heart has paced and paced,
will pace and pace across the field where yarrow
was and now is dust.
A leaf catches in a bone.
The burrow is shut by a tumbled clod
and the roots, up-turned, are hot to the touch.
How my god is a feathered and whirling thing; you will singe your arm
when you pluck him from the air, when you pluck him from that sky where
evil swirls, and you will burn again
throwing him back.

The Sea of Time and Space

But we see only as it were the hem of their garments
When with our vegetable eyes we view these wondrous visions.
— Blake, "Milton"

I.
Midsummer, and a lone bee murmurs among the lavender
along the path we've laid into our garden,
round aggregate slabs that darken in rain
under the feathery leaves of the honey locust
whose lowest branches make us bow.
We have given the body the ritual of its need,
cooked *al dente, putanesca,* in the savory kitchen,
the tulip bowls of our glasses splashed with wine.
Now, in after-dinner twilight still bright above the fenceline,
the compass angle of the house glows against the sky.
In such light, on Peckham Rye, Blake saw his first vision,
the tree above him filled with angels, their wings bespangled
with stars. Thereafter, prophets appeared in the fields
beyond Dulwich and Camberwell, Lambeth Vale;
Gabriel walked with him among the shambles at Carnaby,
his spirit guide through infinite London. And, one day,
God himself gazed from the casement window on Broad Street,
plain as a mother seeking her children in the crowd. . . .
Our ancient days before this earth appeared to my mortal eyes:
inside each particle of dust the elemental strings,
behind the vegetable world the bleak Satanic mills —
gods of his own making, embodied states,
the titan walking behind the carapace of a flea.

II.

Single vision. The earth perceived merely as earth,
devoid of spirit's translucency, its light
dispersed in waves through the sea of time and space,
deranged by the gin of the unaltering eye. . . .
One March morning, after making love, we saw
from our upstairs window a hint of green
among the brown scatter of leaves and wasted fronds
of fiddleheads, the first frail strips of crocuses,
like decorative ribbons, unblooming still,
until earth's economy compounded the scales
in hyacinth and candy-tuft, in phlox overbrimming
the steps, starbursts in the slow motion of its falls.
For weeks we found sprigging among the beds
pliant trunks of infant maples, their outsized
leaves spreading like river deltas, gathering light.
And we'd go uprooting, feeling in our hands the tug
of generation, its mechanism and miracle,
incessant fall of the eternal driven from sweet delight,
unless the mind revive and the body wash itself
of experience. All spring we listened to squirrels
in heat along the powerlines, to the sparrows'
untraceable clamor through the trees.
You soaped aphids from the flutes of honeysuckle,
scattered shards of eggshells under the hostas
to guard them from the slugs you swore you heard
chewing each night through the darkened canopy,
their soft bellies bleeding on quicksilver trails of slime.

III.

In the suburbs of Ulro the mills whirr into motion —
Case, Modine, Twin Disc, plush furnaces of Metal World.
Invisible occupants swag in the burdened clouds.
Their poisons silver the leafage after rain,
sift into soil and skin, ineradicable, then resurrect
in the brute lump seething in the mother's breast.

• • •

Strange smells along the lakeshore, North Beach closed
again beyond the Treatment Plant. Under dead stacks
at Cliffside the church league softballers shout
for their buddy rounding third and heading home.
He has become the idea he longed himself to be
before the grind, and slides safely into reclaimed dirt.

Now, along Franklin Street — call it New Poverty Lane —
under the shadow of the genius's office tower
(his leaking monument to Nature and to Work),
the settled migrant walks beside his ramshackle home,
labors to fulfill the alderman's injunction
to beautify the town or face a fine.

This evening, in the garden, we released the last
of the ladybugs, our small effort at harmony,
their killing a necessary hunger in the balance.
And now, at the feeder, a congregation of birds
pecks at the seed. They bolt, and a jackdaw assumes
the roof, fixed eye unblinking. He caws and caws.

IV.
Today, as though all life existed to amaze us,
a dragonfly alighted on the bench where you were sitting,
gold as though daubed in golden ink, and stayed
a full five minutes, motionless as a brooch.
When Blake descended to his garden, *A Human Wonder of God*,
he'd sit naked with his wife in full view of the street,
as though their bodies had passed into translucency,
light shining through the portal of every pore.
Upstairs, the graver's tools, copper plate and burin,
took ease of their labors in the mind's illuminations:
as though, as though, until what the soul longs for
scores itself within the body's finite bounds.
Playing on their trampoline, the neighbor children shout.
Another neighbor's falcon squawks inside its cage.
Blue globes of thistle shake mildly in a breeze.
The roses, past their bloom, bleed like wax into their stems.

On his deathbed, Blake sang a favorite childhood hymn,
then disappeared, as he said he would, into "The Next Room."
Just now, as if in unison, the fireflies ascended,
emanations of the Mundane Shell, or drifting stars?
No, they are our small lanterns waking with the night.
Just now, just now, and now it is just then.
We might be under water with the bergamot and hyssop.
And the bee remains a pilgrim, aloof and prodigal,
still humming to the engines of his own bright world.

Vessel: *Mythos*

In the beginning was the hand, opposable,
little god's head of a fist,

the star-shape of its mouth — toothless,
sidereal — hurling its curses

into the void. The hand wants to be
an oracle, to bestow

on the world its five-fold wisdom,
glossolalia of wants,

always the eyeless face looking
to strike. *Open, open,*

the prayer goes up. And the god
lies down in its emptiness.

Myth of the Flood

After the voice had made known its intentions,
and the man stood dumb behind the house
he would soon dismantle, board by board
at his wife's dismay, at the neighbor's jeering,
to fashion from its wreckage the saving boat;
after the boat had been filled to bursting
with everything needed to start life anew,
the menagerie's stench fuming in his nostrils,
choking him, a cacophony in his ears
as though he were housing Chaos itself;
after the first slow drops, then the downpour
that made it seem the heavens were oceans,
the jeers turned to pleas, and the pleas in vain;
after The Great Absence, the slow return —
a sudden hush in the bestiary's din, the man
with an olive branch between his fingers,
the waters receding to tranquil streams,
run-offs where the judged lay piled like seaweed,
their bloated bodies steaming on the slopes
and out across the plain; after all that,
as his wife freed the remnant, he made ready
the offering, slaughtered two beasts
who would not make it to the world to come;
then knelt before the pyre while the Power
that changed everything savored the burning flesh.
On the horizon: a warrior's bow thrown down
and shining, a pair of doves arrowing away.
The Power sniffed. The man had his choice of gods.

Hunger for Something

Sometimes I long to be the woodpile,
cut-apart trees soon to be smoke,
or even the smoke itself,

sinewy ghost of ash and air, going
wherever I want to, at least for a while.

Neither inside nor out,
neither lost nor home, no longer
a shape or a name, I'd pass through

all the broken windows of the world.
It's not a wish for consciousness to end.

It's not the appetite an army has
for its own emptying heart,
but a hunger to stand now and then

alone on the death-grounds,
where the dogs of the self are feeding.

Decade

I had only one prayer, but it spread
like lilies, a single flower duplicating
itself over and over until it was rampant,

. . .

uncountable. At ten I lay dreaming
in its crushed green blades.

How did I come by it, strange notion
that the hard stems of rage could be broken,
that the lilies were made of words,

my words? Each one I picked
laid a wish to rest. I mean killed it.

The difference between prayer
and a wish is that a wish knows it will be
a failure even as it sets out,

whereas a prayer is still innocent.
Wishing wants prayer to find that out.

Erotic Energy

Don't tell me we're not like plants,
sending out a shoot when we need to,
or spikes, poisonous oils, or flowers.

Come to me but only when I say,
that's how plants announce

the rules of propagation.
Even children know this. You can
see them imitating all the moves

with their bright plastic toys.
So that, years later, at the moment

. . .

the girl's body finally says yes
to the end of childhood,
a green pail with an orange shovel

will appear in her mind like a tropical
blossom she has never seen before.

To the Reader: Polaroids

Who are you, austere little cloud
drawn to this page, this sky in the dream
I'm having of meeting you here?

There should be a word that means "tiny sky."
Probably there is, in Japanese.
A verbal Polaroid of a Polaroid.

But you're the sky, not a cloud.
I'm the cloud. I gather and dissipate,
but you are always here.

Leave a message for me if you can.
Break a twig on the lilac, or toss
a few dried petals on the hood of my car.

May neither of us forsake the other.
The cloud persists in the darkness,
but the darkness does not persist.

To the Reader: If You Asked Me

I want you with me, and yet you are the end
of my privacy. Do you see how these rooms
have become public? How we glance to see if —

who? Who did you imagine?
Surely we're not here alone, you and I.

I've been wandering
where the cold tracks of language
collapse into cinders, unburnable trash.
Beyond that, all I can see is the remote cold
of meteors before their avalanches of farewell.

If you asked me what words
a voice like this one says in parting,
I'd say, *I'm sweeping an empty factory*
toward which I feel neither hostility nor nostalgia.
I'm just a broom, sweeping.

To the Reader: Twilight

Whenever I look
out at the snowy
mountains at this hour
and speak directly
into the ear of the sky,
it's you I'm thinking of.
You're like the spirits
the children invent
to inhabit the stuffed horse
and the doll.
I don't know who hears me.
I don't know who speaks
when the horse speaks.

The path between

The path between the two twelve-foot hedges
between the fire and the window
hot on the left side   sharp on the right
something wrong   Born wrong
cleaves to itself   deflects you
Still, someone wrote something here in the dirt
and I sip at the word —

The Night Sea

The longing for touch
was what they lived out of
not mainly their bodies

        For that friend
        we walked inside of the night sea
        shedding our skins —

I have lived in your face

I have lived in your face.
Have I *been* you?
Your mother?   giving you birth

. . .

— this pain
whenever I say goodbye to thee

— up to now I always wanted it
but not this

One Foot in the Dark

People forget
don't forget me

                    you
the only white head
in the crowd of young men
live oaks
waiting to be let out of the Visiting Area.

A linnet in the rain

A linnet in the rain
a broken bird-feeder on the branch above her
its roof an inverted V   without any floor
uncradle rocking
In the Visiting Area:
my hand almost touching your hand: ˙
What did we come to learn from one another —

The Passing

The shimmer
gone
out of what we know

Bells
din dan dawn
but we — down here —

You Lord
the needle North
and move the boat

The Art of Distance, I

Wrinkle coming toward me in the grass — no,
fatter than that, rick-rack, or the scallops a ruffle makes,
down to about the fourteenth vertebra. The rest of it: rod
instead of a coil.
                        So I'd been wrong the afternoon before
when the dog, curious, eager to play and bored with me
as I harvested the edge of the raspberry thicket,
stalked it from the back stoop to the lip
of the bank and grabbed the tip
in her mouth and tossed it —
sudden vertical shudder
shoulder-level —
                        wrong
to read survival in its cursive
spiraling back to the cellar window-well
where it had gathered fieldmice like a cat.
And now, if it meant to be heading for the brook,
it veered off-course, its blunt head raised
like a swimmer's in distress.
                        The functioning part
gave out just short of me, inside the shade
but not the bush; the damaged part,
two fingers thick, was torqued
pale belly up, sunstruck.
I left it where it was,
took the dog in, and for hours
watched, from the kitchen window, what seemed
a peeled stick, the supple upper body that had dragged it
now pointed away and occluded by the shade,
the uncut grass.

                    My strict father
would have been appalled: not to dispatch
a uselessly suffering thing made me the same, he'd say,
as the man who, seeing a toad,
catatonic Buddha in its niche, wedged
within the vise of a snake's efficient mouth
clamped open for, then closing slowly down and over it,
bludgeoned them both with the flat side of a hoe.

For once I will accept my father's judgment.
But this had been my yard, my snake, old enemy
resident at the back side of the house. For hours,
the pent dog panting and begging, I watched
from the window, as from a tower wall,
until it vanished: reluctant arrow
aimed at where the berries
ripened and fell.

The Art of Distance, II

My father was an earth-sign and a stoic,
an eldest child, a steward, who took dominion
over the given world — at least, it seemed,
his hundred acres of it, pets we ate,
rabbits minched in the combine, inchling moths
torched in the crotch of the tree to save the peaches.
Scorned excess and complaint. Importuned, said
no, not, can't, never will.
                    What didn't fit
was seeing him cry. He'd stand alone in the field
like a rogue pine that had escaped the scythe,
as he would stand beside the family graves,
a short important distance from the car
where we were hushed until the white flag

had been unpocketed, and he jangled his keys
and got back in, not ever looking at us,

not looking at the brisk instructive face
my mother used on clerks, on amputees.
This all happened long before my mother,
in charge of cheerfulness and world morale,
had lost a body-part and given up —
so it was never in response to her,
the way he wept, or equally the way

he moved through life, one hoof after another:
a sentimental man is singular,
still the boy whose mother's gone away.
The last full day of our last ritual visit —
he'd taken a turn already into the field —
what set him off was hearing the neighbor's gun.
She merely wanted the turtle out of her beans;

he hauled the carcass home, two feet wide,
a rock from the creek, and also elderly
if the shell's whorls correspond to xylem and phloem,
rings we'd count on the cut trunk of a tree.
"Tastes like chicken," he said, gathering
the saw, the maul, chisel, pliers, hatchet
he'd need to unhouse the body and chop it up.

No one wanted to help, or even watch,
except the child intent on the row of knives,
and the child changing her mind with a webbed foot's wave —
dinner was not quite dead — but shudders and tears
were weakness and wouldn't work, jokes wouldn't work
on temper alchemized from noun into verb
as my father pried the armored plates apart,

pale and sweating and silent. And never did he,
sun long gone down, once quit the bloody porch,
the bowl of the upper shell in shards, the entrails

bejeweled with flies, the beaked head, feet and tail
cast off into wet grass, until, at the screen,
holding a platter of meat, he might have been
the Queen's woodsman bringing back the heart.

I heated the oil until it spit at me,
dredged the pieces in flour as I would chicken,
flung them chunk by chunk into the pan.
When chewed undefeated lumps ringed even his dish,
he said I'd done the best I knew, not
naming the skill: deflecting sorrow and terror
into a steady fierceness, and aiming *that*.

The Art of Distance, VI

The enormous world shimmering —
    then, in the magic glass, some of it,
        guessed at, came clear.

Whereas my friend "in nature"
    takes his glasses *off* so he
        "can think." When he says

he thinks with his body — body
    grown substantial over the years,
        as has his thought —

I don't know what he means; or,
    if I do, I think thinking is not
        the body's job,

that the body gets in the way.
    Our friendship feeds on argument.
        Each of us

. . .

has one prominent eye:
      his the one on the right, for the left
         side of the brain,

language and logic; but mine —
      this still startles me — mine
         is the one on the left,

enlarged by superstition
      and music, like my father's more
         myopic eye.

Detachment is my friend's
      discovery, what he commends
         against despair.

And though my father claimed
      I never listen, of course I do:
         after all, who else

but the blind will lead the blind?
      And the years bring their own correction:
         to see a thing

one has to push it away.

Largesse

Aix-en-Provence

Banging the blue shutters — night-rain;
and a deep gash opened in the yard.
By noon, the usual unstinting sun
but also wind, the olive trees gone silver,
inside out, and the slender cypresses,
like women in fringed shawls, hugging themselves,

and over the rosemary hedge the pocked fig
giving its purple scrota to the ground.

What was it had made me sad? At the market,
stall after noisy stall, melons, olives,
more fresh herbs than I could name, tomatoes
still stitched to the cut vine, the soft
transparent squid shelved on ice; also,
hanging there beside the garlic braids,
meek as the sausages: plucked fowl with feet.

Under a goose-wing, I had a violent dream.
I was carrying a baby and was blind,
or blinded on and off, the ledge I walked
blanking out long minutes at a time.
He'd flung a confident arm around my neck.
A spidery crack transversed his china skull.
Then it was not a ledge but a bridge, like a tongue.

From the window over my desk, I could look down
at the rain-ruined nest the *sangliers*
had scrabbled in the thyme, or up, to the bald
mountain in all the paintings. I looked up.
That's where one looks in the grip of a dream.

Linda Does My Horoscope

For Linda Wing

Poets . . . think about fate often if not obsessively. — Charles Baxter

"Let's not *talk* about *my* life, but the Vikings won.
It's a big deal here. In fact, I timed our call — "
"For after the game?" "*And* after the phone calls.
I've never seen a chart with so many retros."
(Retrograde planets, that from earth's perspective
seem to stop in their tracks, and then move backwards.
Ice-masses, recalcitrant, like the heavy atoms . . .)
"Retros mean . . . challenges. They *can* be opportunities.
You don't get things done the way people think they should be."

"Of course, we're not quite sure this chart is right,
if it was War Time — " Permanent Daylight Savings,
part of Prehistory, like transport planes
slowly thrumming over . . . I didn't ask my mother,
I was too embarrassed; besides, I have the feeling
I did once, and the answer was confusing.
"My hunch, knowing you, is that it *is*."

Explanations: intercepted sign, trine, ascendant . . .
The afternoon lengthens, cloudy in both cities,
both alone in our houses . . . I have —
I've had it many times — an odd
clairvoyance of my birth-hour, winter, cloudy, darkening —
not *in* the hospital, but the streets around it —
and a special hush, like . . . I'm afraid, like *Christmas* . . .

. . .

"It's an Aquarian's nature to be hopeful.
An air-sign: gets places by flying. Genius, truth-sayer,
exile. Your Sun and Moon are close —
Sun's your core essence. Moon your emotional needs —
that's good, they like each other. But, Moon in Capricorn — "

"Not great?"
        "No-o. 'Watch out, they want blood,'
this commentator says, but she's an Aries,
they don't trust earth-signs. My mother's a Moon in Capricorn,
it's not all bad. Let's see what someone else says.
'Black-dog depressions.' " "Yes." " 'Deep need for love,
but guarded, paranoid. Not afraid of work.' "
Yes, yes. The years in Arlington, nothing published,
bleakness like antimatter, and wifely silence
palpable, past the study door . . .
"Capricorn moons *accomplish*, even if slowly.
It's a sea-goat, can go anywhere — swim, climb mountains . . .
They're tougher than they look, and do not lose."

"In the seventh house, all this has to do with marriage.
You like weird people — Aquarians do —
but nothing works without the intellectual connection.
Most of all you *need* a mate — though, lacking that,
a best friend will do. You'll spoil people with attention,
charming, but frightening in your dependence . . ."
B. Three weeks, no letter. N.
"Men with Moon in seven devastate women,
they're smart, and soft, and listen, listen, listen.
Placid appearance, inside hysterical —
heart on springs, reacting to how *she* reacts . . ."
Indeed, indeed.

        "Now we come to planets.
Neptune's in Libra, but retro. Your mystical side
develops late, but will help your writing."
Sitting zazen on the stone at MacDowell, forty-three . . .
"Venus in Sagittarius, which she doesn't like,

another hint that love's going to be trouble —
freedom and commitment . . . Nothing at all
in the ninth house, and there should be. It
has to do with ultimate reputation."

So maybe this *isn't* the right chart? Or . . . a blank.

Eleventh house. Gemini. "This is the big one,
ready? You've got a *stellium* here —
three of your big planets, two of them retro,
two asteroids. Mars and Uranus
are closer still, a conjunction." (The Christmas Star?)
"Mars is your boy-planet, drive, combativeness, sparkle,
it's happy in Gemini, and likes Aquarians.
But Saturn, Uranus . . ." They come, the antimatter,
black-hole gravity, majestic, walking backwards,
that sucked years eerily
in, back, or down . . . "Shyness, inhibition."
Nontenure, nonpublication, hinterlands . . .
"Uranus — well, he's called the rude awakener."
Yes, yes. That sense of *meant to be*
that in hindsight, anyway, reconciles mortals
to almost anything.
                              "Pallas near Mars
is auspicious, though — she likes war.
Here's where your Capricorn persistence comes in,
your Aquarian power to grow by leaps.
Trines, too, indicate a happy outcome."

"Trines are good, squares bad?" "Don't *say* that, I'm all squares."

More explanations. I scribble restlessly.
Two hours, my phone bill, on *astrology!*
And yet . . . I half-see them, Pallas and Mars,
swords drawn, like Walsungs, among the heavy atoms
that want blood . . .
                              My mother
once said, you *smiled* so much, as a little boy.

For a moment, my two understandings —
the charmed life, the afflicted life —
come closer than they ever have, a *stellium*.

"Thank you, Linda — you've taken such *trouble*." "You're welcome.
Leos, like me, are lucky for you, but nuts.
Everything in opposition teaches."

It must be almost dark, where you are, already,
like that blessed hour . . . "Time for soup.
I hope I haven't scared you. With those planets,
you wouldn't be alive still if you hadn't
somehow learned from it, and gotten through."

Where the Hills Come Down Like a Lion's Paw on Summer

She'd rewritten her story. I didn't figure
much in it now, or as a means, not an end,
a miscalculation . . . But for me, the high bare hills —
especially that cut, where the power-lines soar out over emptiness —
still seemed the place where I had met with a god,
only a god could erase so much and leave so little . . .
(Though it could comfort, too — as if a blessing
rose from the white dust — when love returned, and hurt.)
I was careful who I took there; but once I took a friend —
a male friend — to whom something so bad happened, so early,
his very interest in the world strikes everyone as a triumph
of life itself . . .
                    It was late October's burnt-orange
before the rains. Coming back, we half-saw something glide
like a shadow over a hillcrest, a carnivore's
low-slung lope, not a deer's.
(There *were* lion warnings.) And then the couple pointing
to the slope behind us, *my* slope, and there they were,
six or eight, leaping twistily into the air
so the snout came down where the tail had been. *Not* lions,
perhaps wild dogs?

                    I'm not
especially brave by myself, but I'll usually follow
someone else who's brave. My friend was off, up the steep
half-track by the fence. They waited
till we were thirty yards away, just close enough
to establish they weren't giving ground, then trotted
over the skyline. But . . . *not* dogs, the ovoid
almost feline ears, yellow fur, the draggly tail . . .
And the curvetting dance? *Maybe they were*
hoping to trick the ground squirrels, my friend said; and ever after
the place seemed half to belong to another god, a god
of twistiness, of survival
under myriad forms.

Tidepools, Part 2

When the second life came from within my body,
at fourteen, fifteen — how I hated this; how I wanted
the Midwest opening

its joyful elm towns
to our returning journey,
like crossed swords above the joyful bride and groom;

its humid light in which things grew so densely
it seemed space could curl inside itself forever
and a birdcall still shoot through, unimpeded —

like a life filled with friends and saying more
unguardedly right than you thought the day had room for,
and more always to step out of the stillness;

. . .

and as the small creatures know they move more safely
for the infoldings,
so at night the dancers, unimpeded,

hardly feeling the need to touch each other . . .
It seemed then one could be mixed with something unknown
by unbetrayable.

It seemed there was an act that was a preparing for death,
and the crickets knew it, with their intermitted
falterless ratchet, down by the grass-stems, near autumn . . .

The moment would come, after years, when they would catch me —
brimming, then stopping; without
measure, without doubt — and the explanation of the world

couldn't hold me more.
They seemed to say, *you have not done your preparing;*
but it is only one action, so there is always time.

The Muse

There she was, for centuries, the big
broad with the luscious tits, the secret
smile, a toga of translucent silk, cool
hand on the shoulder of the suffering
poet — the tease who made him
squeeze those great words out. He
was the mirror *and* the lamp, she the torch
who burned with the blue butane of a pure
refusal, too good for mortal use; her breath
was cold as mountain streams, the chill
of the eternal — no hint of plaque
or any odor of decay. Ethereal as hell,
a spirit in chiffon, the mystery is
how she had got so rounded in the butt
and all her better parts as soft as butter,
why such a wraith should be so ample,
what her endowments had to do
with that for which she set example —
all this was surely Mystery, oh that elusive
object of desire, that "untouch'd bride
of quietness," that plump poetic dish
who lived on air but looked
as if she dined on pasta.

Basta!
A pox on the great Lacan,
who writes with his eraser, on all poetic
Graces, mute and pensive, concave exactly
where he is most extensive — oh look
what she has *not* that he has got,

a thing I'm too polite to mention
except to say it rhymes with Venus,
it was the Latin word for tail;
its root, therefore, is *not* the same as pen,
which comes from the word for feather.

But enough of these fine distinctions.
What a great tradition was born when
Alexander whipped his penknife out, cut
the knot she carefully had tied, leaped
on his mount, a perfect straddle
and let the crotch decide
who was the horse and who was the rider,
who was the muse and who
the writer.

Field of Vision

And if the bee, half-drunk
on the nectar of the columbine,
could think of the dying queen, the buzz
of chaos in the hive, the agitation
of the workers in their cells, the veiled
figure come again to rob the combs —
then would the summer fields
grow still, the hum of propagation
cease, the flowers spread
bright petals to no avail — as if
a plug were drawn from a socket
in the sun, the light that flowed into
the growing field would fail;
for how should the bee make honey then,
afraid to look, afraid to look away?

Epitaph

Though only a girl
the first born of the Pharoah
I was the first to die.

Young then,
we were bored already,
rouged pink as oleanders
on the palace grounds, petted
by the eunuchs, overfed
from gem-encrusted bowls, barren
with wealth, until the hours of the afternoon
seemed to outlast even
my grandmother's mummy, a perfect
little dried apricot
in a golden skin. We would paint
to pass the time, with delicate
brushes dipped in char
on clay, or on our own blank lids.
So it was that day we found him
wailing in the reeds, he seemed
a miracle to us, plucked
from the lotus by the ibis' beak,
the squalling seed of the sacred
Nile. He was permitted
as a toy; while I pretended play
I honed him like a sword.
For him, I was as polished and as perfect
as a pebble in a stutterer's mouth.
While the slaves' fans beat
incessantly as insect wings,
I taught him how to hate
this painted Pharoah's tomb
this palace built of brick
and dung, and gilded like a poet's
tongue; these painted eyes.

Facing into It

for Larry Levis

So it is here, then, after so long, and after all —
as the light turns in the leaves in the old golden
way of fall,
          as the small beasts dig to the place
at the roots where survival waits, cowardly crouching
in the dark,
          as the branches begin to stretch into winter,
freed of their cheerful burden of green, then

   it comes home, the flea-ridden bitch of desolation,
a thin dog with its ribs exposed like a lesson
in mathematics, in subtraction; it comes home, to find its bowl
empty — then the numberless
things for which to be grateful dissolve
like the steam from a fire just doused with water
on a day of overcast grays, lined
by a cold slanting rain —
          it is October, that season when Death
goes public, costumed, when the talking heads
on the TV screen float up smiling at the terrible
news, their skin alight with the same strange glow
fish give off when they have been dead a week or more,
as the gas company adds odor for warning
that the lines may be leaking, the sweet smell of disaster
hanging, invisible, in the air, a moment
before you strike the match —

it is then, brother, that I think of you, of your Caravaggio,
of the head of Goliath swung by its hair,
wearing the artist's own weary expression,
exhausted of everything but its desire
for that beautiful David he used to be; and I think
of all the boys walking the streets
each carrying the severed head of the man

he will become — and the way I bear it is
to think of you, grinning, riding high in the cart leaving
the scene, a pair of huge horses hauling the wagon,
a fine mist rising from their damp shoulders,
unconcerned with what hangs, nailed
to the museum walls — luckily
the fall of Icarus has nothing to do with them,
nor the ruined Goliath who fell like a forest,
nor the wretched Salomes with their blood-splattered
platters, nor the huge stone griffins sobbing
at the gates to Valhalla as the litters are carried past . . .

the dark eyes of the horses are opaque with wisdom,
their hoofs strike the pavements with such a musical decision,
the derisive curl of their lips is so like the mysterious
smile on the angel at Chartres, on Kuan Yin, on the dolphin,
as they pull the cart safe through the blizzards
of Main St., the snow slowly swallowing the signs
though the crossing light beckons —
a soft glowing green like some spectral Eden
in the blank white swirl of the storm.

The stallion neighs once, sends a warm cloud
of breath into the snow-filled air,
and the mare isn't scared yet — at least
she's still pulling. There's a barn out there
somewhere, as they plow through the light's
yellow aura of caution, its warm glow
foretelling what hides in the storm:
a stall full of gold, where the soul —
that magician — can wallow
and winter in straw.

Of a Sun She Can Remember

After they had been in the woods,
after the living tongue woke Helen's
hand, afterwards they went back
to the little house of exile, Annie and
Helen, who had lived in the silent
dark, like a bat without radar in
the back of a cave, and she picked up
the broken doll she had dismembered
that morning in her rage, and limb
by limb, her agile fingers moving
with their fine intelligence over each
part, she re-membered the little figure
of the human, and, though she
was inside now, and it was still dark,
she remembered the missing sun
with a slow wash of warmth
on her shoulders, on her back —
as when you step shivering out of
a dank shade into the sun's sudden
balm — and as the warmth spread,
it felt like the other side of water,
and that is when she knew how
light on water looks, and she put
her outspread hands into the idea
of it, and she lifted the lines of light,
cross-hatched like a web, out of
the water, and, dripping, stretched
the golden net of meaning in the light.

German Chronicle

You can't abandon me
now when I'm dead and need tenderness.
— Zbigniew Herbert

1. Cut Photograph: 1941

My mother cared most about beauty. Its absence
hurt her like sickness, like loss of life.
So she cut the photograph at that place on my father's chest
below the heart where the belly begins, leaving intact
my body, riding his shoulders, and his arms
stretched out above his tanned grin, holding my hands in his hands.
A band of sky and sea behind us — bereft of pounded shells and sand
where we'd been walking — we floated then, relieved
of beach and history with its brutal endings.
For years in the plastic window of my wallet
I carried this proof that beauty lives,
something clipped out of a tangled story and freed,
a world of its own, complete with its own plot:
the tiny rider lifting a man out of the sea
where he is half-submerged. She's pulling him firmly,
her legs slung around his neck: at any moment now
he will emerge, dripping down to his ankles,
and they'll float higher into the cloudless day.

2. Cigarette Case: 1942

When I think of them now, those men
drafted to work for a war they didn't believe in,
I see their gray suits arriving at our house after dark,

hands buried in their pockets. Once the door to my father's room
closed, with the flick of one hand they opened
those sleek silver cases filled with the slim wrapped shapes,
miniature corpses lined up in a row, lit them
all over the room like small funeral pyres, saying some things
aloud and others in whispers — and I, in my father's lap,
crying into his big white handkerchief about my first
pulled tooth, watched as if I already knew
that men can be extracted and leave a space, not only gaping
but blank and dismissive: a lid clicked shut for good —
They knew their turn would come, being not only tools
but targets. They waited and watched the smoke unfurl
across their faces, still young and eager —
Even the spy in their midst was only a man who wanted to live.

3. Eels: 1943

On the Sundays when they emptied the wicker traps
the men would enter the kitchen. Their rubber boots
tracked across the tiles and left them streaked and smeary.
Some brought buckets of salt, some the heavy tubs
of muscled mass, thick as a man's arm, but pliable
as rope and slimy: too slippery for bare hands.
My father with his friends would frost his palms
with salt before he'd lift each dangling beast
and rub down its length of blackish skin.
They scrubbed and rinsed them. They mopped the floor.
But even when they'd driven off to the smokehouse
a sickening smell stayed and trapped our breath.
From the bottom of one tub the cut-off heads would glint
like cold steel buttons on military leather.

4. My Father's Tailor: 1943

His hands at home in yards of fabric,
woolens, flannel, and fine cotton; they were so nimble
he could fix anything. His vests were famous.
He knew how to shape fabric as if it were clay,

as if he could fashion the man himself. And he could tell
the latest gossip in the city of Riga,
holding five pins in the left corner of his mouth.
The last time he came to the apartment
a guard stayed by the door with a gun,
and while he fixed the stove in our kitchen
I watched my mother stuff cigarettes and bread into his baggy pockets.
Her hands were trembling. No words were said.
And after he was gone, she cried
over the little gas wreaths of bluish flame.

5. Five Thousand Head of Cattle: 1944

In some history Baltic refugees recorded,
my father is acknowledged for rescuing
five thousand head of cattle overrun by the eastern front.
Whom else he might have helped or counseled — or
whom he failed — is not recorded, nor what he said or thought.
But there are five thousand cows that made it, thanks to him,
onto a freight train heading west. When I think of them
and their descendants, grazing somewhere near
what was Danzig once or Prussia,
they lift their heads to pause as they chew,
not caring whether they're Polish or German,
and look east with their big dreamy eyes —
then bow their heads down to the grass.

6. Bullet: 1944

When he aimed his revolver, we stood half-way
behind him and held our breath before the still, white hand
with its finger on the trigger. Then we counted the echoes
answering back through the winter night
and touched the wound in the tree where the bullet
had buried itself like a secret grief.
It was his last visit.
We'd coaxed him long enough, a handful of children
walking home through woods more silent now

than they had been. Much later I saw he'd wanted
to please us. Then I wondered whether that tree still stood
somewhere in Austria, if I could still find it. There are moments
when I see myself reaching into the splintered wood
to feel its metal core. Every time,
it singes my finger to the bone.

7. The Radio: 1944

Nobody could remember how he had carried it or why
it hadn't been confiscated, a handsome Blaupunkt
with foreign names printed on the dial's backlit glass
where the needle would wander from Belgrade to Hilversum,
London, and Paris. From the unlit station of some Alpine village
he pulled it on a sled up the mountain. That's how I see him:
a man alone in the snow under stars glinting like distant cities,
his gaze traveling among them as if to ask: Is there
a place to go where one could live? In our room
when we unpacked it the glass was broken, and my mother
assembled the shards like a puzzle. On tracing paper
she copied the cities as bright dots and cut a hole
for the dial knob. Fitted into the walnut frame of the casing
it covered the void that gaped behind the needle,
holding the shattered world in place.

8. Berlin: 1940/1945

I remember nothing of that city but a dead mouse
we buried together, how my mother scooped out a hole
in my grandfather's garden and I placed the small corpse
inside, wrapped in its shroud of maple leaf.
How I filled in the earth until it made a mound
and marked it with a small oval of stones.
Later when we found out about my father,
how he had died in that city, I remembered
that mouse and how my mother had wiped the earth from the ring
on her finger so carefully. Then I saw that soil
on the ring of his hand. And he and the mouse

became inseparable, so when I thought of him walking through the streets
in those last days, there was always a mouse on the sidewalk
scampering ahead like a shadow before him.

9. Cherry Soup: 1945

During a lull two weeks before the end, my father
visited the landlady of his student days in Berlin.
A soldier now, soiled with the grime of trenches and history,
he knocked at her house in the midst of ruins. The first thing
she remembered was his adoration of her sweet cherry soup.
Though bad knees and air raids had slowed the last harvest,
it had been a good year for cherries, and her preserves
were still lined up in the basement next to her makeshift bed.
While he sat by the boarded kitchen window, she scooped out
the thickened juice dotted with fruit, and they talked
of years that had been innocent and sweet —
Behind the window boards the cherry blossoms listened one more time.

10. Medals: 1945

There weren't many, perhaps three or four,
for services in the Ministry of Food.
His dissertation I still keep unread on my shelf:
the breeding and raising of pigs in Great Britain.
Did his study improve the production of German pork?
Or was he by then concerned with cabbage crops and cattle?
What does a country eat during war but cruelty and grief?

My mother kept them in a small box I'd never seen
until the late spring after the snowmelt
and before the occupation. After we walked in the woods
where, with a spoon, we dug a hole under layers of pine needles,
she lifted the lid and let us hold each one of them:
one was enameled, one silver, one had a colored ribbon.
Why couldn't we keep them? Why couldn't we have them
to play with? My sister and I still argued with her while we patted
the soil and moss back in place.

. . .

For a long time we had no news.
Later it seemed we had buried him then.

11. Shame

Children have their own cruelty.
I wanted him to have rescued five thousand men.
I wanted him to have resisted openly, to be hammered in stone.
I wanted his goodness mounted for all to see.
Children want desperately so much
because so little is left of a man who was human.

12. Absence

It is not nothing. Not the cottonwood felled
in the yard, its split trunk hauled away; not
the stump that stayed behind, its white circle ringed with bark —
but those far-reaching branches built on air
that sway and spread as if the mind had its own wind and light:
the ghosts of birds fly through it.

The Pumpkin Tree

Up a lattice of sumac and into the spars
of the elderberry the pumpkin vine had climbed,
and a week after first frost
great pendulous melons dangled like gods
among the bunches of lesser berries
and the dazzled, half-drunken birds.

Then the pumpkins fell, one by one, each mythical fruit's
dried umbilicus giving way in a rush
of gold and a snow of elliptical leaves.
A skull thud, the dull thunk of rupture,
a thin smoke then, like a soul, like dust.

But the last, high up and lodged
in a palm of limbs and pithy branches,
sways now in the slightest breeze and freeze
after freeze caves in on itself
and will, by spring, cast its black

leathery gaze out over the garden
like the mummy of a saint or an infirm
and dessicated pope. Below, where the others fell,
that seed not eaten by winter birds,
one, say, buried in meat and a sheath

of skin, will rise. From its blunt,
translucent nubbin, a leaf trifoliate
and a stalk as succulent as bamboo, it will climb
blithe as a baby Christ up the knees
of the wood it cannot know it is bound for.

About Language

for Jordan

Damn the rain anyway, she says,
three years old, a hand planted on her hip,
and another held up and out
in the mimic of a gesture she knows too well —
adult exasperation, peevish, wild-eyed, and dangerous.
But the mangy stuffed bunny belies it all,
dangling by an ear, a lumpy flourish.

And so again I am warned about language,
my wife having just entered the room
aims a will-you-never-learn look my way
and I'm counting myself lucky. She missed me,
hands to the window, imploring the world,
Jesus Christ, will you look at the fucking rain!

And because this is western Oregon, and the rain
blows endlessly in from the sea, we let out to play
in the garage, where I peer balefully
into the aging Volvo's gaping maw
and try to force a broken bolt, that breaks,
my knuckles mashed into the alternator's fins
bejeweling themselves with blood and grease.

And what stops my rail against the Swedes,
my invective against car salesmen, my string
of obscenities concerning the obscenity of money,
is less her softly singing presence there
than my head slamming into the tired, sagging hood.
I'm checking for blood when I feel her touch my leg.

What tool is this, Daddy? she's asking,
holding a pliers by the business end. Then
what tool is this? Channel locks. And this?
Standard screwdriver, sparkplug socket,

diagonals, crimper, clamp, ratchet, torque wrench,
deep throw 12-millimeter socket, crescent,
point gauge, black tape, rasp —

but suddenly the rain's slap and spatter
is drowned in the calling of geese,
and I pick her up and rush out, pointing,
headed for the pasture and the clearest view.
And rising from the lake, through rain
and the shambles of late morning fog,

vee after vee of calling Canadas,
ragged at first, then perfect and gray and gone
in the distance. They keep coming and coming,
and pretty soon we're soaked, blinking,
laughing, listening. I tell her, they're geese,
they're honking, and she waves and says honk-honk.
She says bye-bye, geese; she says wow; she says Jesus.

Dark Forest

. . . and then, in dreaming,
The clouds methought would open and show riches
Ready to drop upon me, that, when I waked,
I cried to dream again.
— Caliban

I love the way the woods arrange themselves
for my convenience: here's the stob

I hang my pants on and here
the shrub I nestle my still-warm

underwear over, out of each leg hole
a leaf like an almond eye, one black

• • •

fly strolling the vent like a big city boardwalk.
And see how my shirt flung up

is the residue of flame,
a long smoke fading in the weeds.

I hear my boots go running,
though they will not go far down that ravine:

they miss my socks, one fist-size stone
in the toes and thrown.

I'm ready now, dark forest.
Bring on your snakes and bears,

your coyotes singing praises
to my pink and almost hairless flanks.

Bring on the icy night, the cocktail stars,
the flamboyant, androgynous sun going down.

Let my soles go bloody
through the puncture weeds and shards,

let my legs be slashed by thorns:
I will follow my old compass, slouching

toward the north. I will paint myself
in the mud wallows of elk and make my skin

a new brown thing. Give my eyes to the ravens,
my heart to the ungainly buzzard, its head

gone red over all the earth's
uncountable cadavers, liberator of the dust.

. . .

I bequeath my clothes to the unraveling jays
and I will, if I should survive the night,

rise reborn, my opposable thumbs
surrendered to the palms, to find

in a snowmelt puddle a draught
of the same old wretched light,

seeing as the water stills at last
the man I refuse to be.

The Longing of Eagles

No words can tell what they feel, how
mated for life they breed once a year
and no one calls it love, what preening
they do in the last light at dusk,
done for the good of the nest — pure, habitual,
the sweet, uncomplicated essence of instinct.
No gestures pass between them, no eloquent eye
belies a hunger not born of bad fishing,
and the annual surviving offspring blinks once
at its dead nestmate, kicked over the edge and gone.

I do not envy their flights, not climb
or dive or the hover in a hard wind,
outrigger wings gone quiveringly tense.
I do not envy what we call their play,
the swoops and feints, the talons-locked
free-fall tumble in the sun of a false spring.
I do not envy their beauty, nor the keen eye
of the ornithologist, who can tell them apart.
I do not envy the air they fly through,
not the waters that sustain them,

nor the darkness that has made of them
something rare. I do not envy their dignity.

For two weeks now I have watched a single eagle
troll the canyon, and this morning
I found its mate, talons and tail-feathers removed,
a filthy hulk. I do not know if it is male or female,
but I would bet every word I love, the shot
that felled it was fired by a man. I wonder,
as he bent to his work — the hard jerks
at the feathers, the unsheathed
hatchet for the legs — I wonder
if the eyes were open, if even in death
they glared out with that fierce
dispassionate stare of the raptor,
the predator, knowing many things,
but not hatred, not need, not human love.

Sunflower

When Dean Young vacuums he hears
not just time's winged whatchamacallit
hurrying near but some sort of music
that isn't the motor or the attic
or the sucked-up spider's hosannahs
or his mother pounded into a rectangle
or what's inside him breaking
because the only thing conclusive
all those tests showed is inside him
is some sort of crow so unsure of its
crowness, it thinks it's a stone
just as the stone thinks it's
a dark joke in the withered fields
and has to be so opaque to keep
all its ketchupy light inside because
you never know what sonuvabitch
is hanging around, waiting for a chance
to steal your thunder. When Dean Young
has his thunder, nothing moves. Not
the dust in the hose, not the music,
not even the eye of the crow. It drives him
crazy how little effect he has. He thinks
of his friends at ball parks and feels
miserable. He thinks of women's behinds
and feels radiant. He's afraid how he invented
running by moving his legs very fast
will be forgotten, attributed elsewhere.
He can't resign himself to losing the patent
on masturbation. On the other side
of the back of his head hangs his face

which he puts strawberries into.
He dreads strawberries because their mouth
is bigger than his. He dreads his wife
because he loves her. His strong opinions
re: capital punishment, arts education,
the numen dissolve in water,
the universal solvent that falls from clouds,
clouds that were HIS idea.

The River Merchant, Stuck in Kalamazoo, Writes His Wife a Letter During Her Semester Abroad

We were looking forward to being alive.
Now you new place! Me not too! Strange taste
afternoon lonely for hummingbird mouthful.
You somewhere else make everywhere else
elser. I know almost nothing about this flower
growing from my chest. Does it need dead-heading?
Only you not answer. This complete the test
of the emergency broadcast system? Definition
of the female breasts as modified sweat gland
certainly leave out curfew-breaking! Sunny melon
morning all day! Remember! In my dream, almost
get your sash off then wake of sadness. Forceful
but gentle I not girl-scaring want to explain
not like Jim explain his night in jail so
fly-around he explain other nights in jail.
No hello river in the sky then. When someone
love you, good to be afraid-making in that way? Not
nice among dumb bamboo thickets, ga-zillion
crickets not one Thelonius Monk. Ha ha
only so long. I grow cold. Soon snow
fall on the no more factory.

I Can Hardly Be Considered a Reliable Witness

First there was a raffle conducted by silhouettes
then some gaga clangor and the deflection
of not getting what I wanted probably never.
I was trying to write The Indomitability
of the Human Spirit to impress you but
it kept coming out The Undomesticated
Human Spigot, a blowhard stoned soap opera.
I couldn't understand anything and you
were my teacher. The rain bounced off
the up-turned canoes by the man-made lake
and out of the man-made water small bodies
propelled themselves into the nevertheless air.

This I could not do.

I had been worn out by a lasagna.
A train had run through my almanac.
I had gone directly to the small screen.
It was only a couple times I leaned from the window
in that gorilla mask yet of all I have accomplished
and delayed, my deeds in the outback, cradling
the dying wombats, cataloguing every wrong
ever done to me with innovative
cross-references, this is what I'm remembered for:
leaning from a window in a gorilla mask.

It's frustrating,
like hiding stolen jewelry in tubs of lard.
Sure, it works but have you ever tried
to get grease off a broach?
Or geese out of a coach for that matter.
They have to be heavily sedated
and it's weeks before they can even float right.

How I Get My Ideas

Sometimes you just have to wait
15 seconds then beat the prevailing nuance
from the air. If that doesn't work,
try to remember how many times
you've wakened in the body of an animal,
two arms, two legs, willowy antennae.
Try thinking what it would be like
to never see your dearest again.
Stroke her gloves, sniff his overcoat.
If that's a no-go, call Joe
who's never home but keeps changing
the melody of his message.
Cactus at night emits its own light,
the river flows under the sea.
Dear face I always recognize but never
know, everything has a purpose
from which it must be freed,
maybe with crowbars, maybe the gentlest breeze.
Always turn in the direction of the skid.
If it's raining, use the rain
to lash the window panes or,
in a calmer mode, deepen the new greens
nearly to a violet. I can't live
without violet although it's red
I most often resort to.
Sometimes people become angelic when they cry,
sometimes only ravaged.
Technically, Mary still owes me a letter,
her last was just porcupine quills and tears,
tears that left a whitish residue
on black construction paper.
Sometimes I look at used art books at Moe's
just to see women without their clothes.
How can someone so rich,
who can have fish whenever he wants,
go to baseball games,

still feel such desperation?
I'm afraid I must insist
on desperation. By the fourth week
the embryo has nearly turned itself
inside out. If that doesn't help,
you'll just have to wait which
may involve sleeping which may involve
dreaming and sometimes dreaming works.
Father, why have you returned,
dirt on your morning vest?
You cannot control your laughter.
You cannot control your love.
You know not to hit the brakes on ice
but do anyway. You bend the nail
but keep hammering because
hammering makes the world.

ACKNOWLEDGMENTS

Betty Adcock: "Cycladic Figure," "In a Trunk Not Looked into for Twenty Years," "Renovated Zoo, Now Called *Habitat*," and "South Woods in October, with the Spiders of Memory" previously appeared in *Intervale: New and Selected Poems* (Louisiana State University Press, 2001).

Joan Aleshire: "Full Flower Moon" first appeared in *The Nation* and was reprinted in *The Yellow Transparents* (Four Way Books, 1997). "Persephone," "Slipping," and "To Charlotte Brontë" were published in the prizewinning book *This Far* (vol. 27 of the Quarterly Review of Literature Poetry Book Series, 1987). "Slipping" previously appeared in *Poetry* and *Sound and Sense*. "To Charlotte Brontë" previously appeared in *The American Scholar* and *The Pushcart Prize: XIII*. "Up To" appeared in *The Marlboro Review*. "Wide-Eyed Look" appeared in *Virginia Quarterly Review*.

Agha Shahid Ali: "Some Vision of the World Cashmere," "Ghazal," and "The Last Saffron" are from *The Country without a Post Office*, copyright © 1997 by Agha Shahid Ali. Used by permission of W. W. Norton & Company, Inc.

Debra Allbery: "After the Auction of My Grandmother's Farm," "Chequamegon," and "Imaginary" appeared in *TriQuarterly*, a publication of Northwestern University. "Chronic Town" appeared in *Poetry*. "Carpathian Frontier" and "River" appeared in *New Virginia Review*.

Tom Andrews: "Praying with George Herbert in Late Winter," "Reading Frank O'Hara in the Hospital," and "Evening Song" are reprinted from *The Hemophiliac's Motorcycle*, published by the University of Iowa Press, 1994. Used with permission.

David Baker: "Benton's Clouds" and "Ohio Fields after Rain" are from *Changeable Thunder*, copyright © 2001 by David Baker. "Treatise on Touch" is from *The Truth about Small Towns*, copyright © 1998 by David Baker. All are reprinted by permission of the University of Arkansas Press.

Marianne Boruch: "Bad Cello" appeared in *Iowa Review.* "Bones Not of This Puny World" appeared in *American Poetry Review.* "I Imagine the Mortician" appeared in *Field.* "Lament" is from *A Stick that Breaks and Breaks* (Oberlin, Ohio: Oberlin College, 1997). Reprinted by permission.

Karen Brennan: All poems in this volume are published here for the first time by permission of the author.

Anne Carson: "My Religion," "Flexion of God," "God's Name," "The Wolf God," and "God's Ardor," all from the sequence "The Truth about God: Seventeen Poems," appeared in *American Poetry Review* and in *Glass, Irony, and God* by Anne Carson, published by New Directions Publishing Corporation, 1995. Reprinted by permission of the author.

Michael Collier: "Argos," "Brave Sparrow," and "My Crucifixion" are from *The Ledge,* copyright © 2000 by Michael Collier. Reprinted by permission of Houghton Mifflin Company. All rights reserved. "The Barber" is from *The Neighbor* by Michael Collier, copyright © 1995 by The University of Chicago. All rights reserved. "Bardo" appeared in *The Atlantic Monthly.*

Peter Cooley: "The Other" is reprinted from *Nightseasons* by permission of Carnegie Mellon University Press. Copyright © 1983 by Peter Cooley. "For Lear" is reprinted from *Sacred Conversations* by permission of Carnegie Mellon University Press. Copyright © 1998 by Peter Cooley. "Final Season," "My Crow, Your Crow," and "Nocturne with Witch, Oven and Two Little Figures" are from *A Place Made of Starlight* and are used by permission of Carnegie Mellon University Press. Copyright by Peter Cooley.

Carl Dennis: "Gelati," "The God Who Loves You," "A Priest of Hermes," and "Not the Idle" are from *Practical Gods,* copyright © 2001 by Carl Dennis. Used by permission of Viking Penguin, a division of Penguin Putnam, Inc.

Stuart Dischell: All poems in this volume are published here for the first time by permission of the author.

Stephen Dobyns: "How It Was at the End" and "How To Like It" are from *Velocities* by Stephen Dobyns, copyright © 1993 by Penguin Putnam. "His Favorite Blue Cup" is from *Pall Bearers Envying the One Who Rides* by Stephen Dobyns, copyright © 1999 by Penguin Putnam. Used by permission of Viking Penguin, a division of Penguin Putnam, and Harold Ober Associates. "No Moment Past This One" appeared in *Poetry,* May 2001. "(His life was the practice)" is from

The Porcupine's Kisses, copyright © 2002 by Stephen Dobyns. Used by permission of Penguin, a division of Penguin Putnam, and Harold Ober Associates.

Stephen Dunn: "A Postmortem Guide," "Burying the Cat," and "Oklahoma City" are from *Different Hours,* copyright © 2000 by Stephen Dunn. Used by permission of W. W. Norton & Company, Inc. "Poe in Margate" and "Chekhov in Port Republic" are published here for the first time by permission of the author.

Lynn Emanuel: "The Burial," "inside gertrude stein," and "The White Dress" are from *Then, Suddenly—* by Lynn Emanuel, copyright © 1999. Reprinted by permission of the University of Pittsburgh Press. "The Dig" is from *The Dig: Poems,* copyright © 1992 by Lynn Emanuel. Used with permission of the poet and the University of Illinois Press.

B. H. Fairchild: "Old Men Playing Basketball," "All the People in Hopper's Paintings," and "The Machinist, Teaching His Daughter to Play the Piano" are from *The Art of the Lathe,* copyright © 1998 by B. H. Fairchild. Reprinted with the permission of Alice James Books and The Waywiser Press.

Roger Fanning: "Australia," "Faces Underwater," "The Great Gizzardo," "Herkimer, Mohawk, et al., in Autumn," "Lord of the Jungle, Larva-Nude," and "What We Wait for" are from *Homesick,* copyright © 2002 by Roger Fanning. Used by permission of Viking Penguin, a division of Penguin Putnam, Inc. "Australia" first appeared in *The Drunken Boat.* "Faces Underwater" originally appeared in *The Virginia Quarterly Review.* "The Great Gizzardo" and "Lord of the Jungle, Larva-Nude" first appeared in *Parnassus: Poetry in Review.*

Roland Flint: "Bang!" is from *Stubborn: Poems,* copyright © 1990 by Roland Flint. Used with permission of the University of Illinois Press. "Wake," "Spring," and *"Barukh ata adonay"* are published here for the first time by permission of the Estate of Roland Flint/H. Rosalind Cowie.

Chris Forhan: "The Fidgeting" and "Nothing Doing" appeared in *Poetry.* "Gouge, Adze, Rasp, Hammer" appeared in *New England Review.* "The Actual Moon, The Actual Stars" appeared in *Ploughshares.*

Carol Frost: "Komodo," "The St. Louis Zoo," "Compatibility," and "Scorn" are from *Love and Scorn* by Carol Frost, published by Northwestern University Press, Evanston, 1998. Reprinted with permission of Northwestern University Press. "Requin" is published here for the first time by permission of the author.

Reginald Gibbons: "Blue Annunciation" appeared in *Ontario Review*. "Ghazal" appeared in *Luna*. "Down There" appeared in *American Poetry Review*. "I Not I" and "*Envoi*" are published here for the first time by permission of the author.

Louise Glück: "Mock Orange" is from *The First Four Books of Poems*, copyright © 1968, 1971, 1972, 1973, 1974, 1975, 1976, 1977, 1978, 1979, 1980, 1985, 1995. "Celestial Music" is from *Ararat*, copyright © 1990. "The Wild Iris" is from *The Wild Iris*, copyright © 1993. "Ithaca" is from *Meadowlands*, copyright © 1996. "Nest" is from *Vita Nova*, copyright © 1999. Used with permission of HarperCollins and Carcanet Press Limited. Copyrights by Louis Glück.

Barbara Greenberg: "The Education" and "The Visitation" are reprinted from *What Nell Knows* (Summer House Books, 1997). "I Was Looking" and "What They Are" (originally published as "August 27, 1971") are reprinted from *The Spoils of August* (Wesleyan University Press, 1974). "The Education" appeared in *Poetry Northwest*. "I Was Looking" appeared in *Shenandoah*. "The Visitation" appeared in *The Gettysburg Review*. "The Knife Accuses the Wound" is published here for the first time by permission of the author.

Linda Gregerson: "Cord" appeared in *The Kenyon Review*. "Grammatical Mood" appeared in *Joe*.

Brooks Haxton: "I Am" appeared in *Partisan Review*. "Submersible" appeared in *New England Review*. "Sackcloth," "God's World, 1927," "Rotgut," and "Scrolls" are published here for the first time by permission of the author.

Edward Hirsch: "The Desire Manuscripts" appeared in *The Paris Review*.

Tony Hoagland: "Jet," "Lawrence," and "Lucky," copyright © 1998 by Tony Hoagland, are reprinted from *Donkey Gospel* with the permission of Graywolf Press, Saint Paul, Minnesota. "Carnal Knowledge" from *Sweet Ruin*, copyright © 1993 by Tony Hoagland. Reprinted by permission of The University of Wisconsin Press. "Jet" and "Lawrence" appeared in *Ploughshares*. "America" appeared in *American Poetry Review*.

Marie Howe: "What the Living Do," "Practicing," and "A Certain Light" are from *What the Living Do*, copyright © 1997 by Marie Howe. Used by permission of W. W. Norton & Company, Inc. "Prayer" and "Reading Ovid" are published here for the first time by permission of the author.

Laura Kasischke: "Do Not Leave Baby Unattended" from *Fire and Flower*, copyright © 1998 by Laura Kasischke, is reprinted with the permission of Alice

James Books. "Do Not Leave Baby Unattended" appeared in *Georgia Review*. "Joy" appeared in *Southern Review*. "Small Boys Petting Caterpillar" appeared in *Iowa Review*.

Brigit Pegeen Kelly: "Blacklegs" originally appeared in *Tamaqua* and was reprinted in *The Pushcart Prize XXII*. "Elegy" appeared in *TriQuarterly*. "The Satyr's Heart" appeared in *The Kenyon Review*. "Sheep Child" appeared in *Third Coast*. "Sheet Music" appeared in *Salt Hay*. "The South Gate" appeared in *The Recorder: The Journal of the Irish-American Historical Society*.

Mary Leader: "Balm" appeared in *Virginia Quarterly Review*. "Impetus" appeared in *Membrane*. "Linear" appeared in *Denver Quarterly*.

Larry Levis: "Caravaggio: Swirl & Vortex" and "Coda: Kind of Blue" are excerpted from "The Perfection of Solitude: A Sequence" from *The Widening Spell of the Leaves* by Larry Levis, © 1991. Reprinted by permission of the University of Pittsburgh Press.

Thomas Lux: "Henry Clay's Mouth" appeared in *The Atlantic Monthly*. "Bonehead" and "Portrait" appeared in *American Poetry Review*. "Beauty School," "Tactile," and "Pre-Cerebral" are published here for the first time by permission of the author.

Campbell McGrath: "Because This Is Florida" appeared in *The Paris Review*. "Benediction for the Savior of Orlando" appeared in *The Indiana Review*. "The Zebra Longwing" appeared in *The Kenyon Review*. "The Orange" is published here for the first time by permission of the author.

Heather McHugh: "Etymological Dirge" and "Past All Understanding" are from *The Father of All Predicaments*, © 1999 by Heather McHugh (Wesleyan University Press, 1999). Used by permission. "What He Thought" is from *Hinge & Sign: Poems 1968–1993*, © 1994 by Heather McHugh (Wesleyan University Press). Used by permission. "The Looker" and "Just Some" are published here for the first time by permission of the author.

Pablo Medina: All poems in this volume are published here for the first time by permission of the author.

Steve Orlen: "Butterflies That Save Us from Ourselves," "Nature Rarely Confides in Me," and "Reverie: *The Saturday Evening Post*" are from *This Particular Eternity* by Steve Orlen, published by Ausable Press, 2001.

Gregory Orr: "Almost a Loneliness" previously appeared in *Meredien*. "Be-All" previously appeared in *Controlled Burn*. "Bolt from the Blue: A Sequence," "(Trauma) Storm," "Screaming Out Loud," and "How Smoothly . . ." are published here for the first time by permission of the author.

Kathleen Peirce: "Confession 1.8.13" appeared in *Colorado Review*. "Confession 10.8.13," "Ovidian," and "Two Sisters" appeared in *The Paris Review*. "Confession 4.2.3" and "Confession 2.5.10" are published here for the first time by permission of the author.

Lucia Perillo: "Inseminator Man" and "Lost Innocence of the Potato Givers" are from *The Body Mutinies*, published by Purdue University Press. Copyright © 1996 by Lucia Perillo.

Carl Phillips: "From the Devotions," copyright © 1998 by Carl Phillips, is reprinted from *From the Devotions* with the permission of Graywolf Press, Saint Paul, Minnesota. "The Kill," copyright © 2000 by Carl Phillips, is reprinted from *Pastoral* with the permission of Graywolf Press. "Trade" appeared in *Parnassus: Poetry & Review* (2001).

Claudia Rankine: "Section 1," excerpt from *Plot* (Grove Press Poetry Series, 2001), is reprinted with permission from Grove Press.

Kenneth Rosen: All poems in this volume are published here for the first time by permission of the author.

Michael Ryan: "A Good Father," "Every Sunday," "Reminder," and "A Two-Year-Old Girl in a Restaurant" appeared in *American Poetry Review*. "Birthday" and "Wings of the Morning" appeared in *The Kenyon Review*.

Grace Schulman: "American Solitude," "Last Requests," and "Poem Ending with a Phrase from the Psalms" are from *Paintings of our Lives,* copyright © 2001 by Grace Schulman. Reproduced by permission of Houghton Mifflin Company. All rights reserved. "The Present Perfect" is from *For That Day Only* by Grace Schulman. Reprinted with permission from The Sheep Meadow Press, Riverdale-on-Hudson, New York.

John Skoyles: "Front Street" is reprinted from *Permanent Change* by John Skoyles, published by Carnegie Mellon University Press in 1991. "After Surgery," "The Burned Boy," "Definition of the Soul," "History," and "Mop String" are reprinted from *Definition of the Soul* by John Skoyles, published by Carnegie Mellon University Press in 1998. "After Surgery" appeared in *TriQuarterly*. "The Burned Boy" appeared in *Boulevard*. "Definition of the Soul" appeared in *American Poetry Review*. "Front Street" appeared in *Ploughshares*. "History" appeared in *Atlantic Monthly*. "Mop String" appeared in *Virginia Quarterly Review*.

Tom Sleigh: "Augusto Jandolo: On Excavating an Etruscan Tomb," "Prayer," and "The Dreamhouse" are from *The Dreamhouse*, copyright © 1999 by Tom Sleigh, published by the University of Chicago Press. "Newsreel" appeared in *TriQuarterly*.

Dave Smith: All poems in this volume reprinted by permission of Louisiana State University Press from *The Wick of Memory: New and Selected Poems 1970–2000*, copyright © by Dave Smith. "Descending" first appeared in *The Kenyon Review*. "Making a Statement" originally appeared in *DoubleTake*. "Of Oystermen, Workboats" and "Red Dog" first appeared in *The New Yorker*.

Maura Stanton: "At the Vet's" appeared in *Many Mountains Moving*. "Encounter on an Italian Beach" appeared in *Hayden's Ferry Review*. "A Night in Assisi" appeared in *Poetry*. "Tatyana" appeared in *Southwest Review*. "Dead Moth in a Bottle of Mineral Water" and "Lost Life" are published here for the first time by permission of the author.

Susan Stewart: "Let me tell you about my marvelous god" and "The Seasons" appeared in *Stand*. "Two Brief Views of Hell" is published here for the first time by permission of the author.

Daniel Tobin: "Myth of the Flood" and "Vessel: *Mythos*" appeared in *The Bellingham Review*. "The Sea of Time and Space" appeared in *Image*.

Chase Twichell: "Decade," "Erotic Energy," "Hunger for Something," "To the Reader: If You Asked Me," "To the Reader: Polaroids," and "To the Reader: Twilight" are from *The Snow Watcher*, copyright © 1998 by Chase Twichell. Reprinted with the permission of Ontario Review Press.

Jean Valentine: All poems in this volume are published here for the first time by permission of the author.

Ellen Bryant Voigt: "The Art of Distance, I, II, VI" and "Largesse" are from *Shadow of Heaven* by Ellen Bryant Voigt, published in 2002 by W. W. Norton & Company, Inc. Used by permission of W. W. Norton & Company, Inc.

Alan Williamson: "Linda Does My Horoscope" is from *Res Publica* by Alan Williamson, copyright © 1998 by the University of Chicago Press. All rights reserved. "Tidepools, Part 2" is from *Love and the Soul* by Alan Williamson, copyright © 1995 by the University of Chicago Press. All rights reserved. "Where the Hills Come Down Like a Lion's Paw on Summer" appeared in *Virginia Quarterly Review*.

Eleanor Wilner: "Epitaph," "Facing into It," "The Muse," and "Of a Sun She Can Remember" are from *Reversing the Spell: New and Selected Poems*, copyright © 1998 by Eleanor Wilner. Reprinted with the permission of Copper Canyon Press, P.O. Box 271, Port Townsend WA 98368–0271. All rights reserved. "Field of Vision" is published here for the first time by permission of the author.

Renate Wood: "German Chronicle" is from *The Patience of Ice*, published by TriQuarterly Books/Northwestern University Press, 2000. Reprinted with the permission of Northwestern University Press. Selections from "German Chronicle" have previously appeared in *Ploughshares*.

Robert Wrigley: "About Language" and "The Longing of Eagles" are from *In the Bank of Beautiful Sins*, copyright © 1995 by Robert Wrigley. "Dark Forest" and "The Pumpkin Tree" are from *Reign of Snakes*, copyright © 1999 by Robert Wrigley. Used by permission of Viking Penguin, a division of Penguin Putnam, Inc.

Dean Young: "How I Get My Ideas" appeared in *TriQuarterly*. "I Can Hardly Be Considered a Reliable Witness" and "Sunflower" appeared in *Threepenny Review*. "The River Merchant, Stuck in Kalamazoo, Writes His Wife a Letter During Her Semester Abroad" appeared in *Ploughshares*.

Betty Adcock is the author of five volumes of poems from Louisiana State University Press, including the recently published *Intervale: New and Selected Poems*. A Pushcart 2001 prizewinner, she has also received the Texas Institute of Letters Prize for Poetry and the North Carolina Award for Literature, as well as Fellowships from the State of North Carolina and the National Endowment for the Arts. She has been Writer in Residence at Meredith College in Raleigh, North Carolina, since 1983.

Joan Aleshire received a Master of Fine Arts in Writing from Goddard College in 1980. Her first book, *Cloud Train*, was published by Texas Tech Press in 1982 in the AWP Awards Series. Her second book, *This Far*, was published in the QRL Poetry Series in 1987, and her third collection, *The Yellow Transparents*, came out from Four Way Books in 1997. She has won a grant from the Vermont Council on the Arts, a Pushcart Prize, and the Emily Clark Balch Prize from *Virginia Quarterly Review*. She has served as Acting Director in the MFA Program for Writers at Warren Wilson College, and has been a member of the poetry faculty since 1983.

Agha Shahid Ali divided his time between Kashmir and the United States. His eight collections of poetry included *The Half-Inch Himalayas* (Wesleyan University Press), *A Walk Through the Yellow Pages* (SUN/Gemini Press), *A Nostalgist's Map of America* (W. W. Norton), *The Country without a Post Office* (W. W. Norton), and *Rooms Are Never Finished* (W. W. Norton). Translator of *The Rebel's Silhouette: Selected Poems* by Faiz Ahmed Faiz (University of Massachusetts Press) as well as the author of *T. S. Eliot as Editor* (UMI Research Press), Ali received many awards, including Guggenheim and Ingram-Merrill Fellowships.

Debra Allbery's collection of poems, *Walking Distance*, was published by the University of Pittsburgh Press. She lives in Ann Arbor, Michigan.

Tom Andrews's books of poems included *The Brother's Country* and *The Hemophiliac's Motorcycle*. His awards included fellowships from the Guggenheim

Foundation and the NEA and the Rome Prize from the American Academy of Arts and Letters.

David Baker is the author of eight books, including *Changeable Thunder* (poems, 2001) and *Heresy and the Ideal: On Contemporary Poetry* (criticism, 2000). Among his awards are fellowships and prizes from the National Endowment for the Arts, John Simon Guggenheim Memorial Foundation, Ohio Arts Council, and Poetry Society of America. His work appears in *The Atlantic, Double-Take, The Nation, The New Republic, The New Yorker, The Paris Review, Poetry,* and others. Baker resides in Granville, Ohio, where he teaches at Denison University. He is Poetry Editor of *The Kenyon Review.*

Marianne Boruch's four collections of poems include *Moss Burning* and *A Stick That Breaks and Breaks* (Oberlin College Press, 1993 and 1997). Her books of essays, *Poetry's Old Air,* came out in Michigan's "Poets on Poetry" series in 1995. She teaches in the MFA program at Purdue University.

Karen Brennan is the author of *Here on Earth* (Wesleyan), *Wild Desire* (University of Massachusetts Press) and a memoir, *Being with Rachel* (Norton). She is an associate professor at the University of Utah and a regular faculty member of Warren Wilson's MFA Program for Writers.

Anne Carson has written numerous books of poetry and prose, including *The Beauty of the Husband: A Fictional Essay in 29 Tangos* (Knopf, 2001), *Men in the Off Hours* (a finalist for the 2001 National Book Critics Circle award), *Economy of the Unlost* (Princeton University Press, 1999), *Autobiography of Red* (Knopf, 1998), and *Glass, Irony and God* (New Directions, 1995). Her awards include a MacArthur Fellowship (2000), a Guggenheim Fellowship (1998), the Pushcart Prize for Poetry (1997), and the Lannan Literary Award for Poetry (1996).

Michael Collier's fourth book of poems, *The Ledge* (Houghton Mifflin, 2000), was a finalist for the National Book Critics Circle Award and the Los Angeles Times Book Prize. He is co-director of the Creative Writing Program at the University of Maryland and director of the Bread Loaf Writers' Conference.

Peter Cooley was born in Detroit and grew up there and in the suburbs of the city. He has published six books of poetry: *The Company of Strangers* (University of Missouri, reissued by Coyne & Chenoweth), *The Room Where Summer Ends, Nightseasons, The Van Gogh Notebook, The Astonished Hours,* and *Sacred Conversations,* all of which were published by Carnegie Mellon University Press. From 1970 to 2000 he was Poetry Editor for *North American Review.* His newest volume, *A Place Made of Starlight,* will appear in 2003. He is currently Professor of English at Tulane University.

Carl Dennis is the author of eight books of poetry, including *Practical Gods* (Penguin Putnam, 2001), winner of the 2002 Pulitzer Prize in poetry. He has also written a book on the art of poetry, *Poetry as Persuasion* (University of Georgia Press, 2001). In 2000 he was awarded the Ruth Lilly Prize from *Poetry* Magazine and the Modern Poetry Association for his contribution to American poetry. He is professor of English at the State University of New York at Buffalo.

Stuart Dischell is the author of *Good Hope Road* (Viking, 1993), a National Poetry Series Selection, and *Evenings & Avenues* (Penguin, 1996). He has a new collection forthcoming in 2002. His poems have appeared in many magazines, including *The Kenyon Review, Partisan Review, Ploughshares, The New Republic,* and *Slate.* He is Associate Professor of English at the University of North Carolina at Greensboro, where he teaches in the Master of Fine Arts Program in Creative Writing. He has received fellowships from Bread Loaf and the National Endowment for the Arts.

Stephen Dobyns has published eleven books of poems, twenty-one novels, a book of essays on poetry, and a book of short stories (*Eating Naked,* 2000). His most recent book of poems is *The Porcupine's Kisses* (2002). His most recent novel is *Virginal Pursuits* (2002). Dobyns has received a Guggenheim and three fellowships from the National Endowment for the Arts. He has taught at over ten colleges and universities including the University of New Hampshire, Boston University, the University of Iowa, and Syracuse University.

Stephen Dunn's eleventh book of poetry, *Different Hours* (W. W. Norton), received the 2001 Pulitzer Prize in poetry. BOA Editions Ltd. recently released a new and expanded edition of *Walking Light,* his book of essays and memoirs.

Lynn Emanuel is the author of three books of poetry, *Hotel Fiesta, The Dig,* and *Then, Suddenly* — which was awarded the Eric Matthieu King Award from the Academy of American Poets. She has been a poetry editor for the *Pushcart Prize Anthology,* a member of the Literature Panel for the National Endowment for the Arts, and a judge for the James Laughlin Award from the Academy of American Poets. Currently, she is a Professor of English at the University of Pittsburgh and Director of the Writing Program.

B. H. Fairchild's poems have appeared in *The Yale Review, TriQuarterly, Paris Review, Sewanee Review, The American Scholar,* and *The Best American Poems*

2000. His most recent book, *The Art of the Lathe,* was a finalist for the 1998 National Book Award and received the Kingsley Tufts Poetry Award, the William Carlos Williams Award, the California Book Award, the PEN Center West Poetry Award, and the Texas Institute of Letters Award. He has also been the recipient of fellowships from the Guggenheim and Rockefeller Foundations and the National Endowment for the Arts.

Roger Fanning's first book of poems, *The Island Itself,* was a National Poetry Series selection. His new book, *Homesick,* was recently published by Viking-Penguin. He lives in Seattle with his wife and son.

Roland Flint published six collections of poems (*And Morning, Say It, Resuming Green: Selected Poems 1965–1982, Stubborn, Pigeon, Pigeon in the Night,* and *Easy*) and translated several volumes of Bulgarian poetry. He taught creative writing and literature for thirty-six years at Georgetown University, and served as poet laureate of Maryland from 1995 to 2000.

Chris Forhan won the 1998 Bakeless Prize for his first book, *Forgive Us Our Happiness* (Middlebury/University Press of New England). He is also the author of a long poem, *x,* published as a chapbook by Floating Bridge Press, and his poems have appeared in *Poetry, Ploughshares, New England Review, Parnassus,* and other magazines. A native of Seattle, he has been a resident at Yaddo, a fellow at the Bread Loaf Writers' Conference, and a visiting poet at New Mexico State University.

Carol Frost has published two chapbooks and seven full-length collections of poems, including *Pure* (1994), *Venus & Don Juan* (1996), and *Love & Scorn: New and Selected Poems* (2000). Among her many awards are two NEA fellowships and two Pushcart Prizes. Besides the Warren Wilson MFA Program, she has taught at Washington University in St. Louis, Wichita State, Syracuse University, the Vermont Studio Center, the Sewanee Writers' Conference, and the Bread Loaf Writers' Conference. Presently, she teaches at Hartwick College, where she directs the Catskill Poetry Workshop.

Reginald Gibbons is the author of seven books of poems, most recently *Sparrow: New and Selected Poems* (Louisiana State University Press, 1997), *Homage to Longshot O'Leary* (Holy Cow! Press, 1999), and *It's Time* (Louisiana State University Press, forthcoming in late 2002). He has also published a novel, *Sweetbitter* (Penguin, 1996) and other works, including translations of *Selected Poems of Luis Cernuda* (Sheep Meadow, 2000) and Euripides' *Bakkhai* (Oxford

University Press, 2001). He is a professor of English at Northwestern University.

Louise Glück is the author of nine collections of poems and one prose book. She has won the Bollingen Prize, the Pulitzer Prize, and the Bobbitt Prize. She is a member of the American Academy of Arts and Letters and teaches at Williams College.

Barbara Greenberg was an originating faculty member of the Warren Wilson MFA Program. *What Nell Knows* (Summer House Books, 1997) is her most recent collection of poetry. She is currently a Visiting Scholar in Women's Studies at Brandeis University.

Linda Gregerson's most recent book of poetry is *The Woman Who Died in Her Sleep* (Houghton Mifflin, 1996). Her most recent critical book, *Negative Capability: Contemporary American Poetry*, was published by the University of Michigan Press in 2001. She teaches Renaissance literature and creative writing at the University of Michigan.

Brooks Haxton has published six books of original poems and three books of poetry in translation. His most recent book of original poems is *Nakedness, Death, and the Number Zero* (Knopf, 2001). His books of translations published by Viking Penguin are *Dances for Flute and Thunder, Fragments: The Collected Wisdom of Heraclitus,* and *Selected Poems* by Victor Hugo. He is now in his tenth year of teaching at Warren Wilson and in his seventh at Syracuse University.

Edward Hirsch has published five books of poems, including *Wild Gratitude* (1986), which won the National Book Critics Circle Award, *Earthly Measures* (1994), and *On Love* (1998). He has also published two prose books on the nature of reading poetry: *Responsive Reading* (1999) and *How to Read a Poem and Fall in Love with Poetry* (1998). He is a 1998 MacArthur Fellow and teaches in the Creative Writing Program at the University of Houston.

Tony Hoagland has been a member of the Warren Wilson MFA faculty since 1993. His two books are *Sweet Ruin* (1992) and *Donkey Gospel*, which won the 1998 James Laughlin Award. He has received awards from the National Endowment for the Arts and the Guggenheim Foundation. He currently teaches at the University of Pittsburgh, and is working on an essay collection called *Real Sofistikashun.*

Marie Howe has published two books of poems — *What the Living Do* (W. W. Norton & Co., 1998) and *The Good Thief* (Persea Books, 1988), selected by Margaret Atwood for the National Poetry Series — and co-edited with Michael Klein *In the Company of My Solitude: American Writing from the AIDS Pandemic* (Persea Books, 1995). She has been awarded fellowships from the National Endowment for the Arts, the Guggenheim Foundation, and the Bunting Institute of Radcliffe College. She teaches at Sarah Lawrence College and New York University and lives in New York City.

Laura Kasischke's most recent collection of poems, *Dance and Disappear*, received the 2001 Juniper Prize. She has been the recipient of the Bobst Award for Emerging Writers for her first book of poems, *Wild Brides*, and the Beatrice Hawley Award for her third book of poems, *Fire & Flower*, as well as a fellowship from the National Endowment for the Arts and two Pushcart Prizes. She is also the author of three novels: *The Life Before Her Eyes, White Bird in a Blizzard*, and *Suspicious River*.

Brigit Pegeen Kelly teaches in the creative writing program at the University of Illinois, Urbana-Champaign. Her second book, *Song*, was published by BOA Editions, Ltd. in 1995 and was awarded the Lamont Poetry Prize by the Academy of American Poets.

Mary Leader's second book, *The Penultimate Suitor*, won the 2000 Iowa Poetry Prize and was published by the University of Iowa Press in 2001. Her first book, *Red Signature*, was a selection of the 1996 National Poetry Series and was published by Graywolf Press in 1997. Having formerly practiced law, she now teaches at the University of Memphis.

Larry Levis's poetry collections include *The Afterlife, The Dollmaker's Ghost*, and *The Widening Spell of the Leaves. Elegy* (1997) and *The Selected Levis* (2000) were published posthumously by the University of Pittsburgh Press, as was a collection of essays, reviews, and interviews, *The Gazer Within* (University of Michigan Press, 2001). Among his awards were three fellowships from the National Endowment for the Arts, a Guggenheim Fellowship, and an individual artist's grant from the Virginia Commission for the Arts. He taught English at the University of Missouri, the University of Utah, where he also directed the creative writing program, and Virginia Commonwealth University.

Thomas Lux's most recent collection of poems is *The Street of Clocks* (Houghton Mifflin, 2001). He teaches at Sarah Lawrence College.

Campbell McGrath is the author of four books of poetry: *Capitalism* (Wesleyan, 1990), *American Noise* (Ecco, 1993), *Spring Comes to Chicago* (Ecco, 1996), and *Road Atlas* (Ecco, 1999). A fifth book, *Florida Poems,* from which the poems in this anthology were taken, will be published by Ecco/HarperCollins in 2002. Among his awards are the Kingsley Tufts Prize, and Fellowships from the Guggenheim and MacArthur Foundations. He teaches in the MFA program at Florida International University, and lives with his family in Miami Beach.

Heather McHugh is a chancellor of the Academy of American Poets and a fellow of the American Academy of Arts and Sciences. She has taught for stretches at UC Berkeley, the Iowa Writers' Workshop, and the University of Washington in Seattle; but her most abiding devotion is to the MFA Program for Writers at Warren Wilson College, which she has visited as a member of the poetry faculty since it began. Among her works are *The Father of the Predicaments* (poems, Wesleyan University Press), *Broken English* (essays, Wesleyan University Press), and a translation of Euripides' *Cyclops* (Oxford University Press).

Pablo Medina was born in Havana and lived there the first twelve years of his life, then moved with his family to New York City, where his culture shock was softened by snow and by the New York Public Library. He is the author of several works of poetry and prose, most recently *The Return of Felix Nogara* (novel, 2000) and *The Floating Island* (poems, 1999). A recipient of numerous awards for his work, among them grants from the National Endowment for the Arts and the Lila Wallace–Reader's Digest Fund, he is currently on the faculty of the New School University in Manhattan.

Steve Orlen has published five books of poetry. These poems are from his most recent collection, *This Particular Eternity* (Ausable Press, 2001). In addition to Warren Wilson, he teaches in the MFA Program at the University of Arizona.

Gregory Orr is the author of eight collections of poetry, the most recent of which is *Some Notes on Shadows: New and Selected Poems* (Copper Canyon Press). He is also the author of *Stanley Kunitz: An Introduction to the Poetry* (Columbia University Press, 1985) and *Richer Entanglements* (University of Michigan Press, 1993), and co-editor with Ellen Bryant Voigt of *Poets Teaching Poets: Self and the World* (University of Michigan Press, 1997). He has taught at the University of Virginia since 1975, where he is Professor of English and poetry editor of the *Virginia Quarterly Review.* He is also an editor and columnist for the magazine *Sacred Bearings: A Journal on Violence and Spiritual Life,* and has held fellowships from the National Endowment for the Arts as well as the Guggenheim and Rockefeller Foundations.

Kathleen Peirce teaches in the MFA program at Southwest Texas State University. Her most recent book, *The Oval Hour,* was awarded The Iowa Prize and the William Carlos Williams Award, and was a finalist for the Lenore Marshall Prize as well as the L.A. Times Book Award for Poetry.

Lucia Perillo has published three books of poetry, most recently *The Oldest Map with the Name America* (Random House, 1999). In 2000 she received a fellowship from the MacArthur Foundation. She lives in Olympia, Washington.

Carl Phillips is the author of five books of poetry, most recently *The Tether.* His honors include fellowships from the Guggenheim Foundation and the Library of Congress, two Pushcart Prizes, the Morse Poetry Prize, and awards from both the American Academy of Arts and Letters and the Academy of American Poets. He teaches at Washington University in St. Louis.

Claudia Rankine received her MFA from Columbia University and her BA from Williams College. She is the author of *Plot* (Grove Press, 2001), *The End of the Alphabet* (Grove Press, 1998), and *Nothing in Nature Is Private* (Cleveland State University Press, 1994).

Kenneth Rosen is a Professor of English at the University of Southern Maine. He was recently a Fulbright Professor at Sofia University in Bulgaria, and a collection of over fifty of his Balkan poems, *Wonderful Mountains, Dreadful Holes,* is forthcoming from the Ascensius Press of Portland, Maine, which published *No Snake, No Paradise,* and other collections of his poems. Another book, *The Origins of Tragedy and Other Poems,* is forthcoming from the CavanKerry Press of New York. He teaches in the poetry workshop of the Stonecoast Writers' Conference, which he founded in 1980.

Michael Ryan is Professor of English and Creative Writing at the University of California, Irvine. He has published three books of poems (*Threats Instead of Trees, In Winter,* and *God Hunger*), an autobiography (*Secret Life*), and a collection of essays about poetry and writing (*A Difficult Grace*). Among the many distinctions for his work are the Lenore Marshall Poetry Prize, a National Book Award Nomination, a Whiting Writers Award, NEA and Guggenheim Fellowships, and the Yale Series of Younger Poets Award, as well as awards from the Poetry Society of America, *American Poetry Review, Ploughshares,* and *Virginia Quarterly Review.*

Grace Schulman's new poetry collection is *Days of Wonder: New and Selected Poems* (Houghton Mifflin, February 2002). Schulman's earlier books of poems include *The Paintings of Our Lives* (also by Houghton Mifflin, 2001), *For That Day Only, Hemispheres,* and *Burn Down the Icons.*

John Skoyles directed the Warren Wilson College MFA Program from 1985 to 1992, and is currently Chair of the Writing, Literature and Publishing Program at Emerson College in Boston. He has published three books of poems, *A Little Faith, Permanent Change,* and *Definition of the Soul,* as well as a book of nonfiction, *Generous Strangers.*

Tom Sleigh's books include *After One, Waking, The Chain, The Dreamhouse,* and a translation of Euripides' *Heracles.* He has won the Shelley Prize from the Poetry Society of America, an Individual Writer's Award from the Lila Wallace/Reader's Digest Fund, and grants from the Guggenheim Foundation and the NEA. He teaches at NYU and Dartmouth College.

Dave Smith is Boyd Professor of English and Coeditor of *The Southern Review* at Louisiana State University. His most recent book is *The Wick of Memory: New and Selected Poems, 1970–2000* (Louisiana State University Press, 2000).

Maura Stanton received her BA from the University of Minnesota and her MFA from the University of Iowa. Her books of poetry include *Snow on Snow* and *Cries of Swimmers* (both appear in the Carnegie Mellon Classic Contemporary Series), *Tales of the Supernatural* (David R. Godine, 1988), *Life Among the Trolls* (Carnegie Mellon, 1988), and *Glacier Wine* (Carnegie Mellon, 2001). She is also the author of a novel, *Molly Companion,* reprinted in Spanish as *Rio Abajo,* and two collections of stories: *The Country I Come From* (Milkweed Editions, 1988) and *Do Not Forsake Me, Oh My Darling,* recently published by University of Notre Dame Press. She teaches in the MFA Program at Indiana University, Bloomington.

Susan Stewart teaches poetry and aesthetics at the University of Pennsylvania and is a MacArthur Fellow. She is the author of three books of poetry, most recently *The Forest* (University of Chicago Press). Her prose study *Poetry and the Fate of the Senses* is forthcoming from Chicago and her translation, with Wesley Smith, of Euripides' "Andromache" appeared in the new classical tragedy series at Oxford University Press.

Daniel Tobin's book, *Where the World Is Made* (University Press of New England, 1999), was co-winner of the Katherine Nason Bakeless Prize. A book of criticism, *Passage to the Center: Imagination and the Sacred in the Poetry of Seamus Heaney,* has been published by University Press of Kentucky (1999). His work has been awarded the Discover/*The Nation* Award, a creative writing fellowship from the National Endowment for the Arts, the Robert Frost Fellowship of the Bread Loaf Writers' Conference, The Greensboro Review Poetry Prize, and most recently the Donn Godwin Poetry Prize.

Chase Twichell has published five books of poetry, the most recent of which is *The Snow Watcher* (Ontario Review Press, 1998), which won the Alice Fay DiCastagnola Award from the Poetry Society of America. She is the editor of Ausable Press, a new publisher of poetry.

Jean Valentine is the author of eight books of poetry, most recently *Growing Darkness, Growing Light* and *The Cradle of the Real Life* (Wesleyan, 2000). She was awarded the Shelley Memorial Prize by the Poetry Society of America in 2000. She lives and works in New York City.

Ellen Bryant Voigt is the author of six volumes of poetry — *Claiming Kin, The Forces of Plenty, The Lotus Flowers, Two Trees, Kyrie,* a National Book Critics Circle Award Finalist, and *Shadow of Heaven.* She has also published *The Flexible Lyric,* a collection of craft essays, and co-edited, with Greg Orr, *Poets Teaching Poets: Self and the World,* craft essays by Warren Wilson MFA poetry faculty. Founder of low-residency graduate education for writers, she has been the Vermont State Poet, a Lila Wallace–Reader's Digest Writing Fellow, and a Guggenheim Fellow.

Alan Williamson is Professor of English at the University of California at Davis. His most recent books are *Res Publica* (poetry, Chicago, 1998) and *Almost a Girl: Male Writers and Female Identification* (criticism, Virginia, 2001).

Eleanor Wilner's most recent book is *Reversing the Spell: New and Selected Poems* (Copper Canyon Press, 1998). Her awards include a MacArthur Fellowship and Juniper Prize; she has recently been Visiting Poet at the University of Utah, University of Chicago, Smith College, and Northwestern University.

Renate Wood has published two collections of poems, *Raised Underground* (Carnegie Mellon University Press, 1991) and *The Patience of Ice* (TriQuarterly Books/Northwestern University Press, 2000). A recipient of a grant from the Colorado Council on the Arts and the Emily Balch Prize of *The Virginia Quarterly Review,* she has taught at the University of Colorado in Boulder and is presently on the faculty of the MFA Program for Writers at Warren Wilson College, where she earned her MFA degree.

Robert Wrigley's books include *In the Bank of Beautiful Sins* and, most recently, *Reign of Snakes,* which received the 2000 Kingsley Tufts Award in poetry. He is director of the MFA program in creative writing at the University of Idaho.

Dean Young has received fellowships from the Fine Arts Work Center in Provincetown, from Stanford University, and two from the National Endowment for the Arts. He has published five books of poems, most recently *Skid* (University of Pittsburgh Press, 2002). He lives in Berkeley, California, with his wife, novelist Cornelia Nixon, and his cat, Keats.